COWLEY PUBLICATIONS is a ministry of the brothers of the Society of Saint John the Evangelist, a monastic order in the Episcopal Church. Our mission is to provide books and resources for those seeking spiritual and theological formation. Cowley Publications is committed to developing a new generation of writers and teachers who will encourage people to think and pray in new ways about spirituality, reconciliation, and the future.

T0159025

Informed by Faith

A Spiritual Handbook
for Christian Educators and Parents

Mark Francisco Bozzuti-Jones

Cowley Publications
Cambridge, Massachusetts

Published in the United States of America by Cowley Publications, a division of the Society of Saint John the Evangelist. No portion of this book
may be reproduced, stored in or introduced into a retrieval system, or
transmitted, in any form or by any means—including photocopying—
without the prior written permission of Cowley Publications, except in
the case of brief quotations embedded in critical articles and reviews.

Library of Congress Cataloging-in-Publication Data:
Bozzuti-Jones, Mark Francisco, 1966-
 Informed by faith : a spiritual handbook for Christian educators and
parents / Mark Francisco Bozzuti-Jones.
    p. cm.
 Includes bibliographical references.
 ISBN 1-56101-263-7 (pbk. : alk. paper)
 1. Christian education–Philosophy. 2. Christian education–Home training.
I. Title.
  BV1464.B69 2004
  268–dc22
                              2004018693

Scripture quotations are taken from the *New Revised Standard Version* of
the Bible, © 1989, by the Division of Christian Education of the National
Council of the Churches of Christ in the United States of America. Used
by permission.

Cover design: Jennifer Hopcroft

This book was printed in the United States of America on acid-free paper.

Cowley Publications
4 Brattle Street
Cambridge, Massachusetts 02138
800-225-1534 • www.cowley.org

Contents

Introduction

All of us educate, teach, and form others. We do so because we in turn have been educated, taught, and formed. It is a process of formation that we take surprisingly much for granted. Some of us might even deny that we educate, teach, and form others, and others might be surprised to learn that we are always being educated, taught, and formed.

As Christians we accept the role of our community as a place where we learn and are formed. At the end of each Eucharist, we are given a command to go in peace to love and serve the Lord. One aspect of loving and serving the Lord in the world is to be agents of education, teaching, and formation—in the home, in the church, and wherever we move and have our being.

Where does all this educating, teaching, and forming occur? In truth, every waking moment of our lives offers opportunities in these areas. Though everything we see, experience, and do helps in our ongoing formation, at times education, teaching, and formation take on a more formal and deliberate nature. Here, we think of schools, churches, and various other learning communities. But let us not overlook the potential in the home and family for ongoing formation and learning about God, Christian values, and how to be in society.

The home offers a unique opportunity for ongoing Christian formation. Those who teach, preach, and work in Christian formation in the church benefit tremendously by remembering the formative nature of the family. Teachers and religious leaders outside the home support the religious nature and nurture of families by providing family members with opportunities to deepen their spiritual lives. When religious educators help families to understand themselves as a community of faith and friends, then there is greater opportunity for a more radical daily living of Christianity. By reclaiming their roles as disciples and apostles in the home, parents ensure that their children receive a well-rounded religious education.

One of the primary purposes of religious formation in the home is to equip the members of a family to know God, specifically to know that God is a God of life, God is love, and God is a mystery. More than ever our society needs the examples of families that struggle with what it means to know God in their daily lives, loves, and encounters with pain, suffering, and death.

As families explore living together, loving each other, and celebrating each other's mysteries, they are drawn into the realization that other families share their experiences. That realization leads them to seek fellowship with like-minded families, who see in the church the locale of the community of believers. In the community called church, families—in which I, of course, include singles—confirm and reaffirm their decision to follow God.

When families live into their decision of knowing God, they make decisions and act in ways that are based on the belief system they proclaim on Sundays and in their homes. All of us will experience more difficulties living our Christian principles if they are not supported in the home.

The home, considered to be the domestic church, sets the tone for what happens in the church community. As parents and friends in the community of believers, we bring one another to church and offer ourselves through the baptismal covenant to ensure that each newly baptized person grows up in the knowledge of the Christian faith.

The Christian community comprises a variety of individuals and families who commit to one another in the creedal professions, the opening of Scripture, the breaking of the bread, and the challenge to be disciples in the world. As Christians come together, they discover that one of their primary roles is to educate. In educating one another they offer one another the best support possible.

Religious education is a journey that the Christian community makes together. The members of the community educate one another by reminding one another about who God is and what God has taught them through Jesus Christ and the ongoing presence of the Holy Spirit. Teachers and preachers in the church take on primary roles in this journey. Yet those primary roles are always modeled on the life of Jesus, who washed his disciples' feet. Therefore teachers and preachers minister best by listening, sharing openly, shepherding, and remaining open to learning from and being formed by those to whom they minister. As members of the community journey together, they seek always to restore their souls and to be led beside streams of living waters.

The experience of leading and teaching can be quite tiring. Those who journey always enjoy coming to a rest stop, a place where they can eat, drink something warm or cool, take a bath, or just rest for a while. When we have a chance to rest and refresh ourselves, the rest of the journey becomes a more joyful experience.

For this reason I offer a few ideas to act as rest stops for teachers and parents in this community of faith we call the church. My hope is that these thoughts and suggestions will be a map for the journey of education, teaching, and formation. By giving teachers and parents a chance to think and pray, I hope to offer a spiritual map for a spiritual journey. Teachers need time to prepare for their lessons; Christian teachers in particular need to prepare spiritually for their lessons.

Part of such spiritual preparation might be prayer that leads to self-knowledge, knowledge of God, and a deepening relationship with Jesus. A popular saying affirms, "The family that prays together stays together." By inviting you into an experience of prayer, this book will encourage you to share that experience with others as a means of sustenance for the spiritual path. Prayer, the food and drink of spiritual formation, leads us to discover Jesus present among our families and friends, offering us life, love, and the challenge to serve others. This book is bread and wine for the journey, a journey in which the teacher and the parent can discover the presence of Jesus the teacher in everyday life.

Teaching as a Spiritual Undertaking

In this book I hope to create a dialogue among religious educators and parents that will lead to meditation, prayer, reflection, and a new perspective on the ministry of teaching.

This book is a finger pointing to the moon. Of course, one can always search for the moon by oneself, but a pointing finger sometimes makes the journey easier, the goal easier to attain. This is an opportunity to learn some new ideas about religious education in the home and the church. The intent of these pages is to strengthen the partnership between church and home by valuing the important role parents, Directors of Religious Education, and church-school teachers have in the life of the Christian community and the family.

This book is described as a "spiritual handbook" because I believe that teaching in the church is a spiritual undertaking and that those who teach must find ways to engage the Spirit in their own lives. While the book provides information, it also offers teachers a chance for spiritual reflection, formation, and action.

This is not a book to be read in one sitting, but one with which to spend prayerful time. As you read, spend time doing the meditations and jot down your observations or share them with a friend. The object is less to finish the book and more to notice what happens to you as you journey through the book and stop at the rest spots. In that sense I hope that no one will ever *finish* reading this book.

Knowing that many who teach in the church live quite active lives, I want to invite the readers to become *contemplative in action.* In our busy world, we are in danger of losing sight of the holy and losing the sensation of the Spirit in our lives. A parent or teacher who engages in spiritual preparation before and during any tasks will lead by example.

A teacher without faith cannot teach about faith. A teacher who has no experience of God cannot teach about God. A teacher who has not experienced the consolation of God cannot teach about joy. Contemplation brings self-awareness.

That awareness is what allows a teacher to tap into the richness and the poverty of her or his spiritual experiences. Without that awareness, teaching becomes merely a repetition of lifeless phrases. Part of our preparation involves taking the time to be contemplative. In prayer, in spiritual conversations, and in actions that promote justice and mercy, we grow in educating others about the spiritual life.

Most of the chapters in this book begin with a meditation, an invitation to be still before and in the presence of God. By allowing our experience of God to inform our lives, we enrich the lives of those we teach. It is the examined life that gives teaching and learning their worth.

Aware of this, monastic communities have long practiced such daily personal examination. The *examen* is an ancient method of prayer used by Jesuits throughout the world, typically before retiring for the night. In the *examen,* one reviews one's thoughts, words, and deeds of the day, and in so doing, looks for signs of the saving grace of God in one's life. A great *examen* question would be, "How am I experiencing the saving power of grace today?" For instance, I am always grateful when I can call on someone in the office to figure out my computer problems. Usually the person who helps me out with my computer woes sticks around for conversation about the spiritual life. I end up profiting a great deal from such occasional spiritual conversations. At other times a greeting from the person delivering the newspaper serves to remind me to be courteous to others. Those brief encounters keep me mindful of the way God bursts into my life on a daily basis. The *examen* offers the opportunity to *find God in all things.*

As part of this discussion on education, I invite you to try using the *examen* or any other method of prayer that makes you more conscious of God's grace. If we see our role as teachers as foundational to the ministry of the church, it will help us understand the role of prayer and the need to be educated by the church, the Bible, and God. Deepening our awareness of God has the added bonus of deepening our discipleship.

The teaching ministry benefits enormously when we are in touch with what is happening in our heart, soul, and country. More and more, God invites us to be people of knowledge and hope. We know that bad things happen in our world, but we are called to believe that God is present in every situation, somehow redeeming that situation.

A friend of mine was going through a divorce and wanted to quit teaching. I encouraged him to go to spiritual direction, to keep seeing his therapist, and if appropriate to share what he was going through with the youth group. For those young people who were struggling to learn about love and commitment, my friend's ability to share about his loss and pain forever changed their lives. The youth learned from his experiences because he was able to talk about the ups and downs in his life from a Christian perspective and from the viewpoint of God being with him through every moment of his life.

My friend confessed to me that at the time, he was only able to make some sense of what was happening in his life by doing the *examen* at night. He was able to discover how he valued the church, how he needed the church, and what part he had played in the breakdown of his marriage.

So what might we learn about ourselves and about those we teach by praying and using the *examen* regularly? The *examen* can help teachers examine the inner atmosphere or inner landscape of their lives. Attention to the seasons and weather patterns of the inner atmosphere of one's heart can educate a person well beyond what he or she can learn in a university. In a society with ever more emphasis on perfection, religious teachers can share in the important ministry of honesty. Honesty in the Christian life helps those who follow God to know the hope of Christ in failure, weakness, and imperfection.

Teachers who examine their lives and have a habit of prayer are more likely to be hopeful. Hope prevents parents and teachers from feeling that the church and the world are going to hell in a handbasket. Where there is hope, there is more desire to see the Christian journey not as one of perfection, but as one that calls us toward perfection. With this attitude we are less likely to scapegoat our children and students.

When we find God in all things, we can help others do the same. When we are people of prayer, we can more easily teach others about the importance of prayer. When we make responsible choices because of our faith, we inspire one another to believe that faith is important to us. The *examen* and other forms of prayer help us to see our lives as a whole, to see God walking on the waters of our lives in our personal history. By praying and sharing our prayer, we give our children a pearl of great price.

At a church-school meeting, I once asked the children if they had ever seen their parents praying. Nine of the children said no. Although the children came to church every Sunday, they did not understand church participation as prayer. It seems obvious that one of the least seen activities is the activity of prayer. Americans define themselves as a spiritual people, and yet the act of prayer remains foreign, private. Prayer, defined as communication with God, is not even recognized as such by children in church.

Prayer means different things to different people, but what is undeniable is that it is time spent with God as a means of deepening our spiritual relationship.

How do we pray? A famous writer once said to students who came to hear him lecture, "If you want to be a writer, write!" That was purportedly the end of the lecture. This instruction may serve us well when we think about prayer: If we want to pray, all we have to do is pray. And yet we find it so hard to find time to pray. We have swallowed the myth that in order to survive or feel important, we have to overschedule. Part of overscheduling is a belief that we profit from our activities in obvious ways: we lose weight, we get more money, or we get our names or pictures in the paper, for example. Prayer does not offer the glamor of other activities, and so we sometimes forget its importance. We have now scheduled God out of our lives, creating a new species of adults and children who are always tired. The *examen* and other forms of prayer are ways we can take time to educate and refresh ourselves in the presence of God.

By examining our lives regularly, we learn to recognize the holiness of our lives, the holiness in others, the holiness of the world, and the holiness of God. By setting aside time with God, by attending to God in our lives, we refresh our perspective on life.

Using This Book

I recommend spending at least ten to twenty minutes a day reading something spiritual or in silent reflection. To help in this task, at the beginning of each chapter are passages from the Bible, a story, or a proverb. Choose one, read it slowly, think about it, and at the end of your meditation session, read that passage again.

You may choose to write down your experience in prayer or in a poem, or to draw something that reflects your time spent alone. You may choose a passage and try to think about it as you drive to work or during your workday. You can spend ten minutes, a week, or a month on a single meditation, story, chapter, or paragraph. An old spiritual practice involves staying with a word or phrase from Scripture for as long as it speaks to you.

One of the purposes of this book is to draw out from the reader things that may aid in his or her ministry. Prayer and silence give us the opportunity to learn about God and ourselves, to reveal something of ourselves to God, and to be taught by God. When these things happen, we find ourselves more spiritually prepared to be educators in the church.

Though this book is a book of meditations, it is still a handbook on education. Why is there a need for a handbook on education? I have touched on the spiritual need for it, but I would like to add a few more practical thoughts, thoughts that inform the spiritual.

Most church-school teachers and parents have not had the luxury of going to seminary or to theological workshops. I do not belittle seminary training or professional studies; indeed, much of what I have to say comes from my reflection on studies done in seminaries, universities, and professional workshops. Do we need to be seminary-trained or be involved in religious formation to teach church school? Of course not. But the ministry of teaching and formation does require study, prayer, and preparation. We can all learn from one another. And one of the best ways to learn and to teach is to develop the habit of sharing our life stories. Hundreds of people have told me that sharing their personal faith stories with others has been their own means of salvation. Hearing others' faith stories may be the means of salvation for our children and youth. There is great profit in hearing them.

The faithfully lived Christian life, with all its failure, pain, death, joy, and love, has much to teach the theologically trained teacher. Life educates, because life comes from God. Liberation theology grew out of listening to the experience of the poor in Latin America. From the uneducated masses, the church in Latin America heard a new call from God, learned a new way of being church, and refocused its mission: it embraced *a preferential option for the poor.* Education, in this book, is seen as an openness to life: a willingness to listen to life experiences, to share life experiences, to reflect on them, and to remain open to being led by the Spirit of God.

In many ways that example summarizes this book, but let me say one or two lines about the chapters that follow. In section one I will discuss the history of education and see how, as teachers and educators, we can allow the Spirit to lead into ourselves and back out again.

The teacher is called to know how to be aware of God, question God, wait for answers, and imitate God. In section two, I will look at education as life. Education begins at the moment of conception, and education must encompass life. We teach so that our students and we *may have life more abundantly.*

I will look at the educational needs of the family, the child, the youth, and the adult. In section three I will examine what it means to be a Christian. Because much of our focus will be on a conscious living out of the baptismal vows, I will pay close attention to the Christian life as a teaching tool.

My hope is that after these three sections, those who teach will feel refreshed in soul, mind, and body, and will recommit themselves to teaching and proclaiming God's life and love. If at the end of this book, those who teach have a deeper appreciation of their ministry, more self-knowledge, a new commitment to prayer and self-examination, and a desire to keep educating themselves in the art of teaching, I will have accomplished my purposes.

Meditation pause: *Before you continue reading, I invite you to put the book down and reflect on what you have read. What thoughts come to mind from the preceding pages?*

Before going on to read section one, spend some time praying, thinking, or writing about the following questions:
•Where do I find grace in my life?
•How does God inform my life? How does God educate me?
•How do I resist being educated by God?
•Who am I?

Meditation thought: *Lead me in your truth and teach me, for you are the God of my salvation; for you I wait all day long (Psalm 25:5).*

Other thoughts:
•You cannot lead where you have not trod. You can try, but it would be better to tread first, before you lead.
•If you do not like the student in you, it is quite likely you won't like the ones outside of you.
•God's love cannot be taught unless you live it, know it, and celebrate it.
•God desires to teach you and to learn from you.

I

Education, Teaching, and Formation
Imitating God

1 A Selective Historical Worldview of Education

Introductory Meditations

Before we begin this chapter on education, teaching, and formation, I invite you to take a quiet period of meditation alone and reflect on one of the following questions:

- What has been my most joyful learning experience?
- What has been the most painful or challenging experience in my life?
- What have I learned from it?
- Who has been my favorite teacher and why?
- What or who has most influenced my Christian faith?
- What have I learned about God that encourages me or challenges me the most?
- What do I enjoy the most about teaching or formation?

You could spread these seven questions over a week or answer them all in one sitting. However you do it, I encourage you to play and pray with the questions. You might want to come back to them as you continue reading. The time you spend mulling over these questions will richly inform how you respond to the materials that lie ahead on education, teaching, and formation.

After spending time with the questions, I invite you to do the same with the following passages and sayings—reading, praying on, reflecting on, and rereading them. You might find it fruitful to express what happens in prayer by writing a journal entry, a poem, a song, or by drawing images that come to mind.

Wisdom is radiant and unfading,
and she is easily discerned by those who love her,
and is found by those who seek her.
.   .   .   .

One who rises early to seek her will have no difficulty,
for she will be found sitting at the gate.
To fix one's thought on her is perfect understanding,
and one who is vigilant on her account will soon be free from care,
because she goes about seeking those worthy of her,
and she graciously appears to them in their paths,
and meets them in every thought.
     (Wisdom of Solomon 6:12–16)

What is inside you is greater than what is outside you.
     (African proverb)

When Jesus saw
the crowds,
he went up
the mountain;
and after he sat down,
his disciples came to him.
Then he began to speak,
and taught them.
     (Matthew 5:1–2)

You can lead a horse to water, but you can't make it drink.
     (Popular proverb)

A Selective Historical Worldview of Education

Education is as old as humanity itself. Human beings have always engaged in a process of education, one that involves teaching and learning. As soon as a child is born, parents begin to guide the child to the source of food, even though the child may have an instinctive urge to feed. A mother begins communicating love to her infant at the moment of birth and prepares the way for months and years of instruction, nurture, and guidance.

We teach our children how to speak, tie their shoes, set the table, do their tasks, drive, clean the house, study, play, and behave in public. Our simple actions every day involve a great deal of explaining, correcting, inventing, and demonstrating. At the end of each day, most of us have been involved in teaching something, even if informally. From this we can surmise that to be human is to take part in the transforming process of educating and learning, to be both a teacher and a learner.

From a historical standpoint, education seems always to have had a religious dimension. Almost every preliterate society had deities whose demands and liturgies were passed on to other generations through education. As we talk about religious and spiritual formation today, it would serve us well to take a look at historical religious education.

One could argue that the act of creation, from a religious viewpoint, was a process of education. Human beings learned over time that there is a Creator who created out of love, that all created things are called to live in love and harmony, and that human beings are invited to share in the ongoing acts of creation.

Creation and human existence inform the actions of human beings. Those who believe in God as Creator desire to live their lives learning more about God and their fellow human beings by taking their relationships with God and one another seriously. One could say that the religious person lives his or her life in imitation of God.

In many ways education is synonymous with life and creation. Creation from a Christian understanding makes us aware of God as Creator and teacher, because shortly after humans were created, God instructed them, "Be fruitful and multiply, and fill the earth and subdue it; and have dominion over the fish of the sea and over the birds of the air and over every living thing that moves upon the earth" (Genesis 1:28). Through God's instructions humans have a sense of what God calls them to be and to do in their lives.

God creates and educates continually. God calls us, who are made in the image and likeness of God, to share in the work of instruction, teaching, and caring for the whole earth. Our life, therefore, mirrors the nature of God when we live lives that educate others about who God is. Jesus Christ reveals to us more deeply who God is by teaching us about God, and it is little wonder that on the morning of the Resurrection, Jesus is called teacher (John 20:16). It is also noteworthy that Jesus commands his disciples to "make disciples of all nations, baptizing them in the name of the Father and of the Son and of the Holy Spirit, and teaching them to obey everything that I have commanded you" (Matthew 28:19–20).

Life is a call to share in the process of education. Daily we teach in our quotidian activities, and daily we are called to teach the lessons of God's love and life. We learn and teach about God and from God through our church communities, our prayer, our love, and our practice of the faith.

To be comprehensive, education must include all the experiences in which human beings encounter life, one another, other cultures, and the complexities or simplicities of all that is, seen and unseen; of all that exists, known and unknown. Education is life, and the process of life, one might say, is a lifelong process.

Therefore education is eternal, transpersonal, transgender, cultural, individually based, communally based, religious, financial, sexual, moral—covering every conceivable aspect of life. All over the world, at any given minute, education is happening. Like life, education changes; it can be good or bad, formal or informal, oppressive or liberating. For instance, slave owners taught their slaves to be obedient as a means of oppression. Luckily, many of the slaves taught each other the value of rebelling against oppression and mistreatment.

We teach our children to form good habits and to avoid destructive and addictive behaviors. More and more, parents search for healthy ways to educate children about the dangers of alcohol, nicotine, and hard drugs, and how to participate in responsible sexual living. One of my most important values to this day is the value of self-esteem. My mother spent many hours a day reminding me and my siblings to believe in ourselves. She helped us understand the importance of working to achieve what we wanted by having us work for our allowances. We did not have a lot of money, and so she explained to us in tender ways that quality of life did not depend on possessing things.

Education is so integral to life that no one can exist without it. God requires that education form part of human history and salvation, because, after all, this is how we experience God as teacher. God is community, and desires to share love and community with humanity. The story of creation states that God creates humans from a place of community: "Let us make humankind in our image" (Genesis 1:26).

From the earth, God *educed* humanity. It is as though God educated us into being. This is what we glean from our creation: God has led us into being. Shortly after the creation of humans, God consulted with them about the naming of the animals and the order of the world. This is not a debate about what God ordered human beings to do or to be, but it is obvious that God led them out of nonexistence into existence, led them from chaos into creativity, and educated them about their choices in life.

From a Christian perspective, education is at the foundation of our very existence because God drew us out of the soil into relationship with God. We value the act of creation as God's first act of education. In many ways our lives as human beings are nothing more than the passing on of the experience of that created act. We believe in God, who created all things and people, and we share in this relationship of education with and through God. God made us for community, and it is in community that we learn and teach.

With each passing day, we grow in awareness of how our existence is intricately linked to people of other places, cultures, religions, and races. At times we live our lives paying scant attention to that reality, but it is one that holds tremendous importance for who we are and where we find ourselves. Like it or not, we are connected to every human being on the planet.

Recent events have brought the lives of Jews, Palestinians,

Arabs, Muslims, and various immigrant groups onto the pages of newspapers and onto television screens. As Christians we treasure the posture of Jesus that seeks a radical inclusion of all peoples, and so as we imitate Christ, our posture to the *other* is always one of love: "I was a stranger and you welcomed me" (Matthew 25:35). In political and sociological terms, we describe this phenomenon as globalization, while as Christians we describe it as being brothers and sisters in God. As we love and care for one another, we can learn from one another's history and experience. For this reason I would like to take a historical journey that looks at education in ancient and varied cultures.

Keep in mind that in those ancient cultures, long before people knew how to write, education meant passing on survival skills. It meant preserving the life of the culture and the peoples by making tools, understanding the changing seasons, figuring out the role of the divine, planting, and making weapons. The skills used in those ancient cultures offer us the earliest educational styles.

African Education

Much of our thinking on education focuses on Western cultures, ignoring the contributions of Africa. Today, most of what we hear, see, or read about Africa features the negative. In the following pages, I hope to redress some of those negative portrayals by attempting to show similarities with and unique features of the African view and experience of education.

The continent of Africa, a collection of countries that boast rich and diverse histories, offers many treasures for understanding education in our present-day context. Here in America many people trace their roots to the continent of Africa, and this alone is sufficient reason to examine education in the African context.

Surprisingly, the African cosmology and worldview hold a concept of existence that includes the visible and the invisible, spirits that roam the heavens and the earth, the intimate connection among human beings, and all that is, seen and unseen. The African reflections on wars, natural disasters, religious experiences, human experiences, and the mysteries of life have led to a compilation of fables, stories, proverbs, and songs that have shaped and demonstrated the African understanding of education.

Many stories about Africans speak of their ability to keep silent, but what is just as prevalent in the African cultures is their wise use of words to educate. Words have a life of their own. They provoke silence or action, and are always seen as powerful. One's words can change the world, one's life, and the lives of others. Learning the powers invested in words is a primary emphasis of African education.

The prologue of John's Gospel begins with the line "In the beginning was the Word," a phrase that recalls the Genesis account of God's creation of all things. In John, as in Genesis, we are reminded of the power and place of words: God spoke and the world was created; Jesus is the eternal Word of God. The word became flesh and lived among humans is how the writer of John's Gospel describes the new experience of the creation. Throughout the Gospel of John, the writer deliberately and repeatedly refers to Jesus as the Word.

Words have power; they have blood; they can change the essence of things. Words lead to conversion, life, and death. To listen to the spoken word is to participate in a divine experience. Because of their realistic view of life, Africans believe that words can be used for evil, words can bring harm, and words can curse and bring judgment. Though many cultures share similar views, Africans to this day believe in the power of words in a way that we would call superstitious. For instance, Africans believe that words can take flesh and that once spoken, they stay around for days. Words spoken by the right person in the right way can be transformed into a person, an animal, or any desired object. A holy or gifted person can hear and understand the talk of animals, which speak on special occasions in human words.

Words, good or bad, always teach about the past, present, and future. Where Africans differ from many other ancient cultures is in their insistence that everything speaks with one voice. Whatever is taught has to be confirmed in words in the spiritual and physical realms, by humans and animals. As a result of their belief in a unified cosmology, Africans believe that no contradiction can exist because anything worth learning is good for the stars, the trees, the cattle, *and* the village. The spoken word (teaching) and the heard word (learning) form the essence of African education when confirmed on all levels. To disobey an order or a teaching is to face death, so powerful is the mandate that comes from words.

Most African countries live life on a communal basis, and education in the ways of the tribes is a most important element for survival. For many Africans, in the beginning was the *word*—so it is in words that they find life and meaning. Words provide the context and the meaning for their lives in community and in the cosmos. Because words predate human beings, having their origin in the gods, humans always have to obey the words spoken by the leaders.

One of my favorite African stories, told to me by my mother in Jamaica, provides an example of how powerful the use of words is in education:

> A man was returning from his farm. He was very tired, having worked all day. He wanted to stop and rest, but he was taking home a special treat for his children and did not want to delay, lest he arrive after they had gone to bed. As he walked he came upon a skull. Shocked at first, because he had never seen a skull, he dropped everything he was carrying. As he came closer, he felt an urge to talk to the skull. He smiled to himself and looked around; no one was in sight. "How did you get here?" "Talking brought me here. I used to love to talk and loved to make others talk. But I really just could not keep my ideas to myself." The farmer ran back to his village and started to tell everyone about the talking skull. Few people believed him, but some did. Soon word got to the king. The king was a philosopher and also had a desire to know everything that was going on in the village. "There is a skull that can talk? Take me to it." The farmer took the king to the spot, and there the skull lay. The farmer tried everything to get the skull to talk. Nothing happened.
>
> Well, something did happen: the king was so furious that he chopped off the head of the farmer. Commanding no one to move the head of the farmer, the king and the villagers left. When they had all departed, the skull said to the newly arrived head, "What is this? How did you get here?"

African cultures have much to teach us, and certainly can teach us much about education through their use of words and stories. Africans throughout the continent use proverbs, poetry, folktales, stories, and songs as a means of imparting knowledge, structuring society, and passing on their traditions. Africans use stories to tell about the ancestors, guide morality, teach about the gods, and keep the whole African society open to the spirits; they use stories to welcome new possibilities and to be on guard against the evils of life. To this day many tribes throughout Africa rely on the power of storytelling to regulate life in the villages.

African storytelling educates African society about the mysteries of life, the importance of respecting nature, and the moral value of treating the foreigner, the poor, and the old with respect. Stories, for the African, meld the opposing forces of life and teach that fiction is real, that the invisible is visible, and that reason or intelligence have value only inasmuch as they demonstrate a virtuous life based on what one has learned from these stories.

Because words were a natural part of being human, everybody had equal opportunity to be wise and virtuous. For the Africans, all of life's stories were created by God and therefore could teach everybody all they wanted to know about life. By listening to the story, individuals got the message about how to be wise. If the story was the theory, the praxis was seen in how one lived after learning from the story. The true learner integrated the story and the words of the wise ones completely into her or his life. No separation existed between the story and the message. Africans soon learned the importance of hearing a story over and over again, until the story's message found a home in them.

Wisdom was gained by listening. The wisest listener made a commitment to struggle with the riddles, the proverbs, the mysteries, and the twists and turns of the story. For this reason there was tremendous value in hearing the story over and over again, and at times from different teachers. The greatest teacher was the one who could package the most wisdom in the least words and the subtlest of terms. Great teachers encouraged their students to find the best words to share their ideas, to hear the unspoken messages behind the words, to listen and to hear when no words are spoken, and, most important, to learn the language of the inanimate and invisible world.

Each story holds a message; in each story lies a question and a challenge. Knowledge comes from staying with the question; it is the person who seeks the quickest answer who oftentimes gets into the most trouble. One's journey with words or story is a journey for life, a journey that challenges the African to make his heart, soul, and mind a storage place of experience and wisdom.

Africans believe that wisdom often is incarnated in folly. Keep in mind that objects speak wisdom, and therefore the fool also has wisdom to offer. One can learn from mistakes, and something apparently foolish can well be the epitome of wisdom and grace. Hence, the village idiot can lead, save, or teach the village. The wisdom of the fool becomes a message warning the listener never to dismiss what seems foolish without first grappling with it.

For the Africans, it must be remembered, the story is most often told in the context of community, and therefore the wisdom from stories was never meant for individual upward mobility, but as a means of making the life of the community better. Education was seen as ensuring the life of the community, by passing on the culture.

Mothers taught their daughters and sons the community's songs, poems, stories, and many of the rules of life. Young girls learned to cook from their mothers and learned many things about their role as women in African society. Fathers taught their sons how to farm, to hunt, and to take their place as adult men. Those lessons were repeated in the stories.

To listen and to store information were at times just as valued as being a good storyteller. It would be fair to say that the African method of education was primarily teaching the proper use of words. At times one had to ponder words, play with words, ignore words, and, at other times, act immediately on them. Good listeners and effective speakers were often chosen to be the village storyteller, for they knew the power of silence and the power of words.

As literacy evolved through the centuries, some communities in Africa had access to more advanced formal education. Writing, the sciences, architecture, and mathematics spread throughout some countries in Africa. In Egypt particularly, the role of the priest is very special, and the instruction to become a priest is quite arduous. From about 3000 BCE to about 500 BCE, priests in temple schools taught the principles of writing, spelling, chemistry, biology, and mathematics. Those training to become priests had the dual task of memorizing the spoken word and the huge volume of prayers and magic formulas being written by the temple scribes. As the need for accuracy in the prayers increased, priests gave more and more time to memorize all the prayers.

Literate African communities still rely heavily on the word and the importance of the stories as methods of teaching. Poets and storytellers continue to educate the community, even though they have no formal training. Anthropologists today marvel at the wealth of information stored in some of the stories or poems that survive in Africa, and only today are they being written down. Some of the poems give the exact dates of the coronations of kings and record the history of wars and astrological events.

What is distinct in the African community is how stories and music are used as educational tools. In many African communities, elders teach ethics through the spoken and sung word. Not only does every member of the community get involved by listening, but as they listen, they also dance. Dancing provides a means for the individuals to absorb the teaching into their bodies. What would our present-day practice of teaching look like if we incorporated music and dance (or another form of movement) as a method of instruction?

In many African communities, no one person is considered to have a monopoly on the stories, but each family can educate their children at home in the traditions of the society. What the family hears when the tribe gathers is what the family passes on to the children in the home. By its nature, the African story is always community based—given by the community, for the community. African stories build up the individual by building up the community.

Today, many of the stories from Africa serve as a means of liberation and remembering for many descendants of African slaves. Many stories and the forms of storytelling that can easily be traced to countries in Africa can also be heard in the United States of America; in South America, especially Brazil; and in the

Caribbean, especially Jamaica and Cuba.

Africans who encounter descendants of Africans in other countries are usually amazed to discover that the stories they learned in Africa are being told elsewhere as a means of educating children about Africa and about life.

For Reflection:
• How do you share your personal stories with others?
• When do you teach with actions and when with words?
• What similarities exist between your culture or ethnic group and the African systems described here?

Asian Education

Asian education places strong emphasis on the oral tradition and written texts as formal education. This system differs from the African method because literacy and formal education in India and China spread much faster than in Africa. Few people in Asia were able to afford education, and a person who could afford it would have had to leave his family behind and live with a teacher for many years. Informal education, as in all other societies, happened among family members.

The earliest texts in China and India were religious texts. Great emphasis was placed on the intense study and accurate memorization of the material. Much of the education from China and India stresses social harmony, particularly holistic approaches to health and freedom from poverty.

In China, formal education started around 2000 BCE, and stressed the importance of philosophy, poetry, and religion. Unlike education in other parts of the world, where teachers encourage debate and argumentative searching for facts, education in China consists mainly of rote learning and memorization. Students never challenge a text, they ask no questions, but memorize the text in its entirety.

Poetry stands as one of the unique forms of Chinese education. Students are taught to memorize the forms and structure of ancient verses. Unlike what happens in many of the African communities where spontaneity and charismatic recitals show connections to the divine, Chinese instructors teach an ordered verse that reflects the order of not only the universe but also the structure of society. A poem sometimes had up to five thousand words, each word with a particular beat, giving essence to the whole poem. The emphasis given to each syllable holds great importance in the understanding and teaching of the texts.

Confucius (551–479 BCE), a world-renowned Chinese philosopher, offers an insight into the methodology of Chinese education. He believes that everyone possesses the possibility to learn and to be a great teacher. The poorest of the poor have the same chance to learn and progress in wisdom as the child born in a palace. Rich and poor need education to ensure that the mores of the society are observed. In Confucius's view, one learns to be ethical by availing oneself of education, because one could not devise an adequate morality on one's own.

The practical sayings of Confucius offer an insight into the emphasis of common sense in daily life. Take, for example, this famous saying: "Those who use their heads will rule; those who use their hands will serve." Here Confucius offers all those who wish to learn a chance for upward mobility. Spoken in a country where for centuries hardship and suffering had disabled the livelihood of many, the saying suggests that education offers a way out. Confucius offers philosophy to all who want to learn, enabling them to see through the hypocrisy of their rulers and to choose an alternative approach to life. At the same time, Confucius challenges the powerful by questioning their policies that insist on a hierarchical society to the detriment of the poor.

Wise men hold a special place in the Chinese culture and establish schools that require students to spend up to fifteen years under their care. Parents take their boy child who demonstrates certain traits of wisdom at a young age to the school of the wise man and leave the son with the wise man. In many ways Chinese parents offer their children as sacrifices for the good of the wider culture and the love of education. Here we see one of the earliest trends of individual education, so different from the African emphasis on community. There is less of a sense of individual learning for wisdom's sake in the African tradition because there was no desire to separate an individual from the community.

India offers a different picture of education because of the caste system that prevents certain groups from having access to formal education. Imagine a system in which it is the norm not to offer education to certain groups. Though the segregated school system in America gives us some understanding of this situation, India was much more intense in its segregation. There, only priests and village leaders could learn the ancient hymns to the gods. As early as 4000 BCE, priests and village leaders sung ancient hymns containing formulas for healing, love, and sacrifices. Education in India in its early form mirrored much of what was happening in other cultures throughout the world, the exception being that the very poor had no access whatsoever to education. In other societies poor people, through good fortune or the benevolence of the rich, might have had a chance to study. Circa 1200 BCE Indian priests taught the sacred texts of Hinduism, as well as science, grammar, and philosophy.

The Veda, sacred Hindu hymns to the gods, was a collection of hymns, prayers, and liturgical formulas. It held the philosophical underpinnings of the Hindu holy life. To be a holy man, one had to study these rubrics and wise sayings, in order to know them perfectly, teach them, and live them. The aristocracy chooses the holy person who will study the Vedic hymns.

It is easy to see the impact this would have on the method of education, because education's sole purpose was to maintain the status quo. Only rulers, soldiers, and priests have access to education, and priests are often chosen because of their willingness to abide by the rulers' wishes. The religious or political leader is the one with the power, and unlike the system in Africa, wisdom was not to be shared with the masses but is that which separates the masses from the elite.

In Asia the availability of education has changed, and is no longer as restricted as we sometimes believe. With the advent of the Buddhist monasteries, many poor men and women found a place of refuge from an oppressive society or caste system and devoted their lives to the study of the ancient truths of Buddhism.

Buddhists describe their method of education in eight parts:

right understanding, right thoughts, right speech, right action, right livelihood, right effort, right-mindfulness, and right concentration. All these require attention to the self and to one's relations to others. By practicing right living through paying attention to one's mind and one's physical reaction to events, Buddhists teach that a person can approach Nirvana, perfect truth and bliss.

Buddhists study and learn about monastic life, but also learn much about the folklore of the great holy men and women. The story or folktale became part of the formal learning of holy men and women, as a means of passing on wisdom. The use of stories served as a way of bringing enlightenment to a learner. Mantras, a few words or sentences with spiritual content or intent repeated many times, were also part of the Asian method of meditation.

Much of religious practice in Asia focuses on the practices of virtue, concentration of the mind, intensive analysis, and at times an intense ascetical approach to the body. Religious teaching and lessons on detachment and constant awareness of emotions, thoughts, and actions prepare the student for life. It is common to discipline the body through fasting, flagellation, and physical work. Many of the religious leaders in Asian culture attempted to teach a way of arriving at truth and enlightenment, ultimately to find freedom from the teacher.

In the seventh and eighth centuries CE, monks throughout Asia established monasteries for more formal training and for the passing on of tradition. The monasteries in Asia functioned as universities. Students were drawn to particular monasteries because of the reputation of the head monk or nun. Nuns or monks who distinguished themselves in holiness or wisdom were sure to draw a large following. In comparison to Jesus, who was more deliberate in his calling of disciples, disciples sought out their masters. Also, Jesus spent considerable time as an itinerant preacher, whereas in the monasteries, disciples, for the most part, lived enclosed and separated from society.

Discipleship focuses more on personal enlightenment, whereas in Christianity the followers of Jesus seek more to transform the world and less to advance in personal holiness. Jesus calls his followers to be in relationship with one another and with

God. In Christianity discipleship rests on being in relationship and in developing relationships in community. Education in the Asian tradition has an independent focus, in which an individual masters the terrain of the soul and becomes self-sufficient.

Human beings today owe much to the Asian system of education. From it we have learned ancient ways of meditation, sculpture, mathematics, chronology, and astronomy. Today many Christians have adopted the styles and ways of Asian monks as a way of enhancing their prayer. Today's interest in Buddhist principles that include a way of praying, eating, and ethical living form a strong part of the lives of many who are disenchanted with Christian life. Many of the Buddhist and Hindu practices of meditation and Confucius's proverbs and sayings are quite popular in today's culture, for example, the saying that it is better to light a candle than to curse the darkness.

For Reflection:
- Read Luke 18:18–25, the story of the rich young man who asks Jesus what he needs to do to inherit eternal life. Jesus tells him to go and sell all he has and give the money to the poor.
- Is ethical living solely dependent on observing the law, or more on a just relationship to the poor?
- List five important life lessons you have learned that inform your relationships with others.

Greek Education
In many quarters ancient Greece serves as a model for formal education. Homer's epic poems, the Sophists, Plato, and Aristotle created a system of study, thought, and education. The foundation that those educators and philosophers set up through their teaching laid the basis of Greek society. Education in Greece varied from state to state, with some states believing that only military education had value. The Greek system of education influenced how education is conducted today, and the thoughts of the Greeks still serve as important currency for theological and political thought, long after Greece lost its political clout in the world.

Greek society was divided into two main sectors: freed citizens and slaves. Among those groups existed multiple subgroups ranked according to place of birth, gender, and resources. Only free citizens attended school; indeed, in some states educating a slave was punishable by death. Free citizens needed education in order to understand the laws of the land and to develop in such a way as to witness to the ethical principles of the individual and the state. Education was geared toward the formation of a strong, safe, and intelligent society that had distinct places for the gods, rulers, men, women, and children.

Women received education, but it was left to the mercy or laws of individual states or men. There was a system of public and private schools in Greece, and many women were educated at home. Women received instruction as a way of making them better servants at home, and athletic training in the hopes that they would give birth to healthy and athletic sons.

For the Greeks, education was predominantly seen as a nurturing of the young men, who were to be trained in the knowledge of the gods, the wisdom of the ancients, the politics of the motherland, the culture of their ancestors, and the ethics of daily living.

Nothing was more important to Greek society than to ensure that the young, especially the boys, were educated and nurtured in such a way that they could take their rightful places in society. In a culture in which the people adored the leaders as quasi-gods, education served as the only way to ensure that leaders were equipped to appropriately defend, protect, and govern the state.

In the 400s BCE, a group of wandering teachers called Sophists taught logic, grammar, and rhetoric. The emphasis of their form of education was to win debates and to argue well one's cause. Out of the work done by the Sophists came Socrates, who sought to change the emphasis of education from winning debates to more ethical pursuits. Socrates (469–399 BCE) stands supreme as one of the most noted and respected Greek educators. He believed that each human being had an embodied knowledge of the good, the true, and the beautiful. The soul or spirit of the human person can reveal truth if it reflects on its experiences. Courage, prudence, justice, and other virtues come through the soul's experience of knowledge and reason. There is no knowledge without knowledge of the truth or even a love for the truth. Socrates encouraged those who would purse the truth to know that truth was always elusive. Because of its elusive nature, truth requires ongoing attention, steadfast care, and self-scrutiny.

For Socrates truth and knowledge existed in everyone, but in many it often remained dormant. To engage the mind in a way that led an individual to discover truth independently of the teacher was the greatest way to teach: this was Socrates' view. Care of the individual and love of the soul, especially its reasoning potential, were essential parts of the Socratic method of education. Christian education maintains a similar emphasis on care of the individual and love of the soul (see Matthew, chapter 25).

Socrates wrote nothing down, believing instead in the power of the spoken word. He educated his followers by encouraging them to wonder about truth, question reality, and engage their teachers with questions. Socrates trusted the thinking process of his audience, and believed that each person, when engaging the words and questions of life, could come to knowledge, especially of how to live the virtuous life.

The love of knowledge and the search for perfection hold sway as a lifelong commitment. Each revelation or learning leads to further questioning, and students had to learn to trust themselves and to live into the mystery of the questions. How unlike our education process today, in which students demand answers and educators often settle for rote responses! One solution for change in the church's understanding of knowledge would be to encourage students to live the questions and the mystery of life. Instead of us being too willing to impart our knowledge of God, we might encourage the young to share their experiences of meeting God in the world by telling their stories.

Truth, beauty, and justice reside in each individual, and Socrates saw his role in the world as leading the truth out of his listeners. The role of the listener was to pay attention and engage the question.

One could say that Socrates believed in a shared experience of the divine. Ultimately anyone could teach and come to the truth. Socrates believed that the gods assisted anyone that they chose to become more learned. The assistance of the gods was not dependent on the person's financial or social status, but solely on the person's humility and willingness to learn. This argument met much resistance from the authorities, the political institutions, and especially the schools of his day. They understood that teachers and students had clear, interactive roles in educational settings. On the other hand, authorities and institutions had the role of preserving tradition and discouraging criticism of the status quo. For the authorities, all knowledge had to confirm their power and authority. Socrates believed that a student could become greater than his master, but, for the leaders of his time, no individual could become greater than the leaders, unless that individual were born into a certain family and selected by them. Socrates believed that the only authority was reason. It is not surprising, therefore, that he met his death at the hands of the authorities. How many of us are willing to experience death in the church because of what we teach?

In 387, Plato, a student of Socrates, brought a new interpretation to the experience of learning and education. Whereas Socrates believed that truth resided in each person, Plato added his own interpretation to Socrates' teachings. For example, Socrates had a greater appreciation of democracy and the equality of all human beings in society. Plato had a love of rhetoric and its ability to persuade others. The truly educated, for Plato, were those who could persuade others with concise, intricate, and well-detailed arguments. For Plato, all virtues emanated from one idea. The universal is linked to the particular, in Plato's understanding of education; it is a striving to attain the good, the true, and the beautiful. For Socrates true knowledge was self-knowledge; for Plato true knowledge existed in seeking the harmony of all things. In Plato's view of the ordering of society, the educated are the ones to rule society.

For Reflection:

• Read Matthew 16:13–17, where Jesus questions the disciples about what people say about him. Finally he asks them who they say or think he is. His questions serve as a way of teaching them about who he is.

• How do you use questions (even those that arise in your heart) as a way of learning or discovering new things?
• How do you discover who you are?

Jewish Education

The Jewish tradition, from which Christianity finds life, has a rich deposit of stories used to educate. I begin this section with a story, as a means of illustrating how stories were used as educational devices for the Jewish people.

I invite you to read this story several times, each time assuming the role of a different character. Then respond to the questions that follow the story.

> The Lord sent Nathan to David. He came to him, and said to him, "There were two men in a certain city, the one rich and the other poor. The rich man had very many flocks and herds; but the poor man had nothing but one little ewe lamb, which he had bought. He brought it up, and it grew up with him and with his children; it used to eat of his meager fare, and drink from his cup, and lie in his bosom, and it was like a daughter to him. Now there came a traveler to the rich man, and he was loath to take one of his own flock or herd to prepare for the wayfarer who had come to him, but he took the poor man's lamb, and prepared that for the guest who had come to him." Then David's anger was greatly kindled against the man. He said to Nathan, "As the LORD lives, the man who has done this deserves to die; he shall restore the lamb fourfold, because he did this thing, and because he had no pity."
> Nathan said to David, "You are the man!" (2 Samuel 12:1–7)

• *How do you deal with the truth about yourself?*
• *When has a story or parable taught you about how you are strong or weak?*
• *What five characteristics best describe who you are?*

For Jews the education process is much like this story about David. Nathan the prophet tells David a parable that has everything to do with the events of David's life.

David becomes engaged in the parable on the level of the mind. His heart is disconnected because he is too caught up in a rational interpretation of the parable and misses his place in the story. He falls into the trap of an overeager student who too quickly assumes that he or she knows the answer.

From David's response, it is obvious that he did not allow his soul and heart to enter into the story. If he had, the prophet would not have needed to point out that David was the man being talked about.

How often we in church hear the parables and the events recorded in the Bible and think that they are referring to other people, other events—something not connected to us! We read in the newspaper about greed, robberies, assaults, and racism, and fail to see that we are all guilty of these sins.

All the events in life, written or spoken, seek to engage us, to lead us out of ourselves, out of our comfortable place, to truth. But we often refuse to be educated, refuse to be engaged.

Jews engage in education by standing before the Torah, like Moses before the burning bush. To stand before the Torah is to listen to it with reverence. With diligent frequency, a Jew must read the Torah alone and in community.

By punctuating their lives with passages from the Torah in this way, Jews take special care to remember God's law daily: "Keep these words that I am commanding you today in your heart. Recite them to your children and talk about them when you are away, when you lie down and when you rise" (Deuteronomy 6:6–7). This was a command of God for the individual and the community.

Reading the Torah stands as one of the highest duties and goals of the Jew. Along with that is the task of allowing the Torah to interpret the life of the community and to give it meaning by unmasking the individual and the community.

Education in the Torah is to be led into a new place where God can say: "You are that man, that woman. You are my people." The Jew reciprocates this activity of God by engaging the Torah to the point of finding God in it and being able to say, "You are the 'I AM,' you are that God."

Jewish education is intrinsically linked to the Torah, because in the Torah, Jews see all that they need to form on earth a priestly and holy people. Unlike many Christians who view the Jewish religion as missing an important event—Jesus as God—Jews believe that in the Torah they have a perfect guide to God.

The Torah is all a Jew needs to be a child of God, to live in the world, and to experience the fullness of the one God here on earth. A Jew educates himself or herself by dialoguing with the Torah in a process of personal and communal enrichment.

At the same time, the community interprets the Torah to find new life in a changing world. Rabbis spend their lives debating aspects of the Torah, making it a living tradition. The Torah is life, and it has life for the Jew because of the educational engagement that each Jew brings to the Torah.

To understand better the educational approach Jews take to the Torah, it is important to realize that there is a Torah with a capital *T* and one with a small *t*.

A Jew learns both the Torah and the method of torah, which is to engage the Torah. Arguing with each other and especially the Torah is a respectful educational method for the Jews.

To engage the Torah with questions and arguments is to pay it the highest respect. Nothing can replace the Torah, not even the new insights or interpretations that may come from the arguments or questions one poses to the Torah.

In summary, a Jewish understanding of the Torah promotes education by drawing out appropriate questions and answers. Passing on the tradition is the definition of *torah.*

Like the Greeks and the Africans, Jews embraced the responsibility to hand on their traditions from one generation to the next. For the Jews it was important to pass on the traditions found in the Torah, because engagement kept them holy, and taught them how to live, how to structure their society, and how to remain true to who they were.

In the Torah, Jews not only found laws but stories and proverbs, things that delighted them and showed them God's love for them.

We saw that the dialogues of Socrates showed his belief in the gift of reason embodied in the individual. By contrast, for the

Jews the Torah possesses the mind of God, which seeks to engage the heart, soul, and strength of not just the individual Jew but the whole community.

Like the African stories, it is not just the story that matters, but the message and the context of the telling. Each storyteller brings a fresh message, not so much because of who the story-teller is but because of the uniqueness of the audience that is engaging the story.

Knowledge of God comes from allowing the wisdom of the Torah to increase the knowledge of the community of seekers who encounter God in the Torah. The Torah is always viewed as being addressed to the ears and hearts of the community. This was its sole purpose.

Jewish education is not a once-in-a-lifetime event; it is continuous and it grows from dialogue with the Torah. The Torah is seen as inexhaustible, with the potential to continuously renew those who engage it.

From dialogue with the Torah, new truths and experiences give life and wisdom to the Jews. Engagement with the Torah creates a rich and ongoing dialogue with their traditions. Ongoing interpretation of the Scriptures and life evaluation make for a more discerning approach to life. Orthodox or Reformed Jews pay close attention to the Scriptures and evaluate their meaning in light of today's experience. To this day the bar mitzvah and bat mitzvah celebrations insist on the child knowing the Scriptures and beginning a lifelong dialogue with them.

As teachers and learners of the Scriptures in the Christian tradition, we can learn much from the traditions of those who preceded us across many cultures. We are called to be a people in dialogue with the Scriptures, called to be a people who question our tradition, but above all we are called to be a people who know the traditions of our faith journey.

2 Talking the Walk of Religious Education Today

Introductory Meditations

Before going any further, ask yourself what your thoughts are on the Greek, African, Asian, and Jewish understandings of education and its methods. What do you find most appealing? What stories from your childhood have you found most educational? How do you engage the Bible?

Choose your favorite Bible passage, read it a few times, and add four sentences to it. The four sentences should come from your imagination, as you try to get in tune with what God might want to say to you. Then pick a passage from the Bible that you find most troubling. It may be a passage on sexuality, murder, poverty, or punishment; make sure it is a passage that disturbs you. Then change the tone or the meaning of it by writing a four-sentence commentary. For example, to "May his children be orphans, and his wife a widow" (Psalm 109: 9), you may choose to add, "Lord, you later taught us to love our enemies. Though I am feeling really angry right now, I know this is not what I wish for this person. So . . ." Remember that one of the purposes of this book is to deepen awareness. We all have passages that make us uncomfortable; if we do not, perhaps we are not engaging the Scriptures as much as we think we are.

After you have finished this exercise, look over the following story and think about how Kathleen is educating her mother and how the mother is educating Kathleen. In your attempts to educate others or yourself, how do you try to control the outcome? How do you stifle the spirit of creativity, and what excuses do you give for doing this? How do you deal with discipline?

Kathleen's mother took her to the shopping mall.

"Mom, may I go watch the magic train?"

"No, darling. You may get lost; I want you to stay beside me."

"Mom, may I buy an ice cream?"

"No, dear. You have on your good blouse; you might get it dirty."

"Mom, may I buy a book?"

"No, Kathy. That bookstore has things that I don't think a little girl
should see."

"Mom, may I play with those children?"

"No, it is good to be by yourself sometimes."

Kathleen began to cry.

The mother started screaming at her, "For God's sake, can't you act
like a grown-up?"

    (Adapted from a story told to me by Tony de Mello)

*Before we continue talking about education, I invite you to do the fol-
lowing meditation:*

*Read Exodus 3:1–6. Meditate on this passage by imagining yourself
as Moses. Use your imagination to feel the heat in the desert, to experience letting the sheep do their own thing, to be fascinated by the
bush, to take off your shoes, and to hear the voice of God. Try to
place yourself in the story as Moses. Think of it as a film about Moses
meeting God in the burning bush, the only difference being that you
are Moses. Spend about fifteen minutes on this meditation. You might
want to take notes, share the experience with a friend, or write a
poem about it.*

Talking the Walk of Religious Education Today
A few thoughts on and definitions of education:

An education is a means to get rich.
An education prepares a person for life and death.
Education is all about learning.
Education is about change.
Education is liberation.
Education is freedom.
Education gives us values.
Education is life.
Education is death.
Education has many goals.
Education changes with the times.
Education is fun.
There is one kind of education.
Education may take many forms.
Education is a divine act.
Education is a human act.
Education is just for children and youth.
Education has lost its usefulness.
One can get by without an education.
Education is useless in today's world.
Education has many challenges.
There is too much talk about education.
The government does not see education as a priority.
The church does not see education as a priority.
Education has nothing to do with God or religion.
I have an education.
I consider myself educated.

I invite you to spend time with these definitions. I have been collect-
ing responses from around the world. What would you add to the list?
What would you subtract? Mark your five favorite definitions. Mark
the statements you disagree with or do not like. Take some time to
reflect and pray about your responses. I encourage you to return to
this section as you read the rest of the book.

Most of us would define *education* as the act or process of educating or being educated, meaning the development of character or mental powers. The verb *to educate* means to give intellectual, moral, and social instruction: it is to provide education for someone over time, to give information, and to train or instruct for a particular purpose.

The etymology of educate is the Latin word *educare,* from which we have the English verb *to educe. Educe* means to bring out or develop from latent or potential existence; to infer or elicit a principle, number, or thought from data within. Education, then, is the process of leading out, the calling forth of wisdom.

Wisdom is experience and knowledge combined with the power of applying our experiences and knowledge critically or practically in our daily activities. In today's lexicon, there is less talk about wisdom than in previous times. It is rare to hear someone described as a wise person, but for many Christians, wisdom is still celebrated as the primary gift of the Holy Spirit. In the Christian community, wisdom is treasured as the gift that gives us an understanding of who God is and what we are in relationship to God and the world:

> For wisdom is more mobile than any motion;
> because of her pureness she pervades and penetrates all things.
> For she is a breath of the power of God,
> and a pure emanation of the glory of the Almighty;
> therefore nothing defiled gains entrance into her.
> .   .   .   .
> For God loves nothing so much as the person who lives with wisdom.
> (Wisdom of Solomon 7:24–25,28)

In the Christian community, we believe that everything good comes from God. It is God who gives us the ability to know. It is God who gives us wisdom. It is God who gives us even the desire to know God. As God increases our desire to know God, we open ourselves to receive more gifts from God that help us to make the most of our lives here on earth. God educates us through the process of gifting us. Because we grow in the realization of God's gratuitousness, we soon learn that there is nothing we can do to deserve God's love. This indeed is the first lesson we learn in our relationship with God: God loves us unconditionally.

As we nurture our relationship with God through prayer and participation in the Christian community, we open ourselves to receive all the gifts that God has in store for us. Christians believe that along with wisdom, we receive grace to live our lives ethically in service of God and others. So those who search for knowledge see God as the author of every good thing.

God's gifts to us are free, given to aid us on our life journey and in our relationships with others. Because God's gifts are free, no one person, church, religion, or society has a claim on God's gifts, especially the gift of wisdom. We therefore can never claim to have all the answers or a monopoly on understanding the ways of God. Recognizing that God's gifts are freely given to all is an aspect of Christianity that is often overlooked. When we forget that God gives freely and to whom God pleases, we commit acts of hate and oppression that have painful consequences.

Children, youth, adults—all people—receive the gift of God's wisdom. This is the starting point for any attempt at religious education or formation: to know and believe that all are gifted in and with the wisdom of God.

So it is important to state again that those who educate in the church attempt to recognize, stir, and lead out the wisdom of God that is present in each person, student and teacher alike. Teachers have the mandatory task of proclaiming that God loves the world and graces the world with many gifts. "For God so loved the world that he gave his only Son, so that *everyone* who believes in him may not perish but may have eternal life" (John 3:16, italics mine).

Educators have the unending task of drawing out of themselves and their students the wisdom that abides within them. Christian education in the church community points inward as a way of helping those who listen discover the gift of God within them. The tasks facing the church community that is informed by faith lie in the ability of the community to find new ways of helping others discover how much God loves them and how God gives them all they need.

All of us fall short of accepting that God's gift of wisdom is just as much alive in the other person, especially in those we attempt to teach. For instance, when we teach children about God, we tell them that God loves them, but once they become teens and adults, there is not much talk about God's love. We forget that knowing that God loves us is just as important for teens and adults as for little children. Once I asked a catechist to invite her adult class to sing, "Jesus loves me, this I know, for the Bible tells me so." She promptly told me that it would be too silly to ask adults to sing a children's song. I then asked her how she teaches God's love to the adults. She told me that adults want to know the meaning of life and not about God's love.

It seems to me that unless the Christian community affirms God's love, then the community has no way to understand the gifts of God. It is true that we need to find age-appropriate ways of talking about the gift of God's love, but too often we overlook the power of God's love, and jump to more complicated areas of the Christian life. The first movement of education in the church needs to be grounded in the love of God. Christian education is the means of allowing everyone to get in touch with the indwelling wisdom of the Holy Spirit, which is the presence of God. By being aware of the Spirit within, we can best cooperate with its prompting.

Each student or learner possesses thoughts, responses, lived experiences, and words that burn with the wisdom of God. Like the burning bush, students and teachers have a fire burning within them, a fire that refines and calls each person to respect the activity of wisdom in the other.

A sign of inherent wisdom is the recognition of the need for education. To desire to be educated shows a thirst for life, for wisdom, and for God. Teachers who acknowledge their need for wisdom show that they do not have a monopoly on wisdom. I was invited a few years ago to meet with church-school teachers in a parish. Before I accepted the invitation, I made them promise that they would invite church-school teachers from neighboring parishes. "Do you mean other Episcopal parishes?" the coordinator asked me. "Not necessarily," I said. "Feel free to invite the Lutherans, the Roman Catholics, and the Methodists." There was silence on the other end. I was sure she was going to tell me that she would find someone else to come and talk to the teachers. "Are you there?" I finally asked. "Yes," she said. And then, "Wow, I had never even thought of finding out what goes on in the church school of these parishes." She promised to invite them. On the night of the meeting, three representatives from each of the neighboring churches showed up. After prayers, I asked the teachers to introduce themselves and answer the questions: "What inspires my teaching? Where do I find God in my teaching?"

Teachers listened to each other and took copious notes, and asked each other questions about the challenges of teaching in the church. When teachers learn from one another, they recognize the holy wisdom in one another. As the evening progressed, it was obvious that the shared wisdom of the group, which came from different experiences in the same field of education, was bearing much fruit. The teachers got a lesson in education by drawing out of one another the joys, frustrations, and strengths of teaching. By the end of the meeting the teachers were in tears. Many of them thanked me for allowing them to encounter places in their hearts and ministries with which they had gotten out of touch.

At the end of the meeting, I challenged the teachers to meet together as a group in a couple of months, and further asked them to invite some of the children to their meeting. One of the teachers piped up that it might be good to ask the students what they liked about church school and what they were learning.

Frequently we teach without getting feedback from our students. If truth be told, the present structure of church school does not allow teachers the opportunity to get to know their students, much less to ask them their opinions of what the experience of being taught is like for them. Wisdom needs a two-way conversation to be true wisdom. When education offers reflective feedback and an opportunity for students to "talk back live," the process of education is guaranteed to be a source of wisdom and knowledge. In honest conversations, teachers and students stand open to the conversion of their hearts, the goal of religious education.

All of us hold treasures of wisdom about our experience of the divine in our daily lives. Yet, the way we are taught in church makes it appear that we are all village idiots. The wisdom of teaching is helping people discover that God is at work in every moment of their lives. To journey down the road of wisdom by admitting our dependence on one another in the learning process mirrors what we know of God's relationship with the people of God and the prophets.

Let us spend some time looking at Moses and his experience of God. Like Moses before the burning bush, students and teachers stand before each other in a reciprocal relationship. God wanted to use Moses to free the Israelites, and Moses needed to know the power of God, the name of God, and the mission of God. Moses' encounter with God was one in which God educated him and God was educated by him. I am not sure how many theologians and biblical scholars would agree with my view of this relationship, so let me explain why I believe that Moses and God engaged in mutual education.

Note that Moses already knew about the oppression of the Israelites at the hand of the Egyptians. So when God calls Moses and tells him about the oppression faced by the people, it was not news to Moses. By paying attention to the story of Moses, we recognize that time and time again, Moses teaches God about the stubbornness of Pharaoh and the people of Israel. God insists that Pharaoh would listen; Moses insists otherwise. God seems to speak of the people of Israel as wanting to worship Yahweh; Moses points out to God that the people are actually quite stubborn. In the dialogue Moses learns much about God, and God learns much about Moses. Both God and Moses grow and change, but one thing does not change: their commitment to each other. Though at times it seems that God will destroy the people and Moses will abandon his vocation, both support each other in the moments when they feel most like giving up. This is a wonderful model of the teaching ministry and the teaching of wisdom.

God's revelation to Moses met, encountered, and embraced Moses' revelation to God. In truth, there is no theophany without human revelation. Human history is the meeting and learning from God, and so is divine history.

There is no education without a student and a teacher, not much education without receptivity, no leading without someone to be led, no teaching without learning, no true student who is not a teacher, and certainly no true teacher who is not a student. And if I may be so bold, there is no God without human beings—this ultimately is the reason for the Incarnation of Jesus Christ, God made man.

Jesus becomes the fullest manifestation of God's teaching activity. At the Resurrection Mary Magdalene meets Jesus at the tomb. Her grief is not lost on Jesus, and when he called her name, "She turned and said to him in Hebrew, 'Rabbouni!' (which means Teacher)" (John 20:16). This must be one of the most tender moments in the Scriptures. Jesus proves to Mary in this encounter that he is the Risen Lord, and Mary reminds Jesus that humans will always experience him as Teacher. There is no God without humanity, because there is no humanity without God. Jesus is God. Jesus is human. Humanity and God are one. In Jesus we see and find the ongoing education of Christian humanity.

The encounter between Mary and Jesus speaks of a mutual encounter of education. We belittle Mary if we fail to see that she is teaching Jesus how much he is remembered, mourned, loved, and celebrated. We also belittle Jesus if we fail to see that he teaches her in that encounter that God is the God of life and the God who witnesses to life. When our process of education is dynamic, exciting, and reciprocal, we imitate the experience of Jesus' teaching ministry.

In the process of education, the dialectic element gets lived out in teachers owning their roles as students and in students owning their roles as teachers in a reciprocal, exciting, and dynamic way.

Notice that when Mary meets Jesus on that Resurrection morning, she wants to cling to him, but he teaches her that what she learns from him must be shared:

> Do not hold onto me, because I have not yet ascended to the Father. But go to my brothers and say to them, "I am ascending to my Father and your Father, to my God and your God." Mary Magdalene went and announced to the disciples, "I have seen the Lord"; and she told them that he had said these things to her. (John 20:17–18)

Education is dynamic because it imitates life. Like Mary, education announces life to others. The life that education announces always comes from an intimate encounter that draws on the wisdom that comes from a relationship of trust and love. In the same way that God sent Moses, Jesus sends Mary. Likewise God sends us to each other to teach about the wisdom of God manifested in the heart of each of us. Encountering God is a dynamic process, and the mission of God is just as dynamic and exciting.

Our needs and history differ from that of Moses and Mary, but God meets us nonetheless, and the lessons we learn from God and God learns from us are also different, but just as much in need of telling. One of the most urgent needs facing the church community today is the need to help adults know that they are capable of teaching or telling others about God. Part of this stems from an inability to claim our wisdom and experience of God. Everybody has the capability to be a teacher, if each person is willing to get in touch with her or his experience of meeting God.

Human beings are constantly changing, and God continues to work through and with the changes. Paying attention to how we experience our changes and God's changes helps us to articulate a way of teaching about God. Here are five questions that might help prospective teachers launch their teaching careers:

• *When did I first learn about God?*
• *What did I first learn about God?*
• *Who has taught me most effectively about God?*
• *Which passages in the Bible speak to me the most?*
• *How can I talk about these experiences in my own style?*

Christian education requires a reflective life that allows the individual to get in touch with the inner movement of the Spirit. One of the ways the Spirit moves in the human heart is to question the answers that exist there. It is in this daily and dynamic experience that teachers are formed, if they can trust their daily encounters with God. In many ways the book of our life experience is all we need.

Awareness of what happens to us in life is a powerful tool of teaching. It is as though our life experiences were a textbook. In this book we learn, like Mary and Moses, that the experience of God always leads us to share with others, always leads us to teach others. When we pay attention to how God is educating us through our experiences, we get a handle on what it means to be true teachers and disciples.

Education is a dynamic process because our experiences remain far from static and it is in these experiences that God meets us. Dynamic education requires grappling with the motivating forces, physical or moral, that educate or inform who we are. As we learn about ourselves and God, we might be called to change, but even change is a part of who we are. We change every moment of the day, and therefore it is helpful if we begin to appreciate the changes we go through as part of the conversion that God calls us to undergo.

Standing before God with who we are and how we act leads to change. When we live into the experience of being who we are and allowing God to be God, life teaches us new things in surprising ways. Being in relationship with God deepens our understanding of who we are and who God is. Examining the relationship of the people of Israel and the life of Jesus, we see that the element of surprise accompanies the process of conversion. Again, it is vital to claim that a part of education is its dynamic nature, how things change.

Take a look at what happens to Jesus in this passage:

> Just then a Canaanite woman from that region came out and started shouting, "Have mercy on me, Lord, Son of David; my daughter is tormented by a demon." Jesus had had a long day of preaching and defending his ministry. He had been preaching about the essence of our relationship with God, trying to convince his hearers to pay attention to what is true worship. Then here comes this woman, a foreigner, as if to test him. Jesus tells her, "I was sent only to the lost sheep of Israel." But the woman is not deterred, and Jesus also does not give in to the wishes of his disciples, who want to send the woman away. So the woman rejoins, "Lord, help me." Jesus, in one of the harshest sayings recorded, says, "It is not fair to take the children's food and throw it to the dogs." Recognizing something deeper in Jesus than Jesus himself realizes, the woman presses on,

"Yes, Lord, yet even the dogs eat the crumbs that fall from their master's table." Then Jesus praises her faith and heals her daughter immediately. (Adapted from Matthew 15:22–28)

Teaching from the places where life surprises us is a powerful way of doing religious education. An element of surprise is ever present and it requires that those who labor as educators be open to changes. Seeking the moments when God learns from us offers delightful surprises. But to do this, we may need to rethink our concept of God. God is dynamic and just as open to change as we are.

This forces both educators and learners to challenge the structures that would insist on uniformity and the status quo. Many of us can identify with the frustration in our parishes or schools when we come up against the wall of "we have always done it this way." How we read the Scriptures, how we worship, how we teach, how we include children, and what we teach are all up for grabs. Music, drama, poetry, and dance are possible ways of teaching the Gospels, but alas, few of our communities are actually willing to take bold and exciting steps.

The educational process is exciting because it opens up new possibilities, new boundaries, transporting the willing individual beyond his or her psychological, spiritual, emotional, and intellectual boundaries. This is often painful, but every mother will tell you that there is no birth without pain.

Often we adults want to keep the excitement level down. Yet, education demands that we awaken the passions of the students, all the passions. As with any good gift, there are challenges, and that is why the educator has to be grounded and confident in her or his journey of awakening. One of the greatest church-school teachers I know is a former hip-hop artist. He uses his past experiences in the classroom. He sings the gospel in hip-hop style. At first the parents wanted me to get rid of him, but I refused. Soon young people from all over the neighborhood started showing up on Sunday for church school. This teacher embodied the change, self-actualization, and excitement that are possible in contemporary religious education.

Let me share another example. A church community called

me in to talk about why people were not attending adult education programs. When I looked over the offerings, I knew why. I gave them the task of asking the people what they would like to learn about or do at church. Then we came up with a new list of educational offerings. The church offered drama, poetry, spiritual writing, yoga classes, spiritual aerobics, reggae, spirituality, and counseling. These courses were guaranteed to get people excited enough to want to attend. Soon there was not enough space to hold the people who were showing up for the offerings. Sometimes all we need to do is to think outside the box.

Excitement should not be repressed, but rather encouraged and challenged. If nothing exciting ever happens in the teaching process, then maybe it is time to quit.

Looking at pain, dealing with boredom, evaluating methods, and taking breaks are ways to ensure that education remains exciting. When we prayerfully reflect on our excitement, we ensure that it is of the Spirit. A church community that once called for my help boasted about its Confirmation class—the kids were having a lot of fun, the teacher told me. Yet, as soon as they were confirmed, they abandoned the church. As I helped that church community think through what had happened, we discovered many things. It was clear that although the children had been having a good time, they were not feeling any more connected to the church. They enjoyed one another's company, and once they knew that classes were over, they had no desire to go to church or to do anything with the wider community. That church community learned a lesson about not just providing excitement but also connecting the children to the church community. Apparently, when the teacher had tried having the kids attend services in the past, they told her that church was too boring. That was the children's excuse to remain isolated, and when their program was over, never to return.

Education is reciprocal because we live interdependent lives. We need one another, because as a Jamaican proverb states so well, "One hand can't clap." Those who educate have the task of making their students see the connectedness of life.

This is only possible when teachers work at being appropriately connected to their students. In the learning process, educators must care about the inner happenings in the lives of the students, and to do this properly, education demands that the teacher be willing to share his or her inner life. That is the reciprocal nature of education.

Education, by its very nature, sets up a complementary relationship in which the student needs the teacher and the teacher needs the student. Both drink from each other's well. Education requires an examined and appropriate thirst for what students have to offer, and if students detect this in the teacher, they will begin to see ways of quenching their thirsts.

Nobody drinks only water or milk, as good as they are. Teachers who open up the thirst for knowledge in students must be prepared to allow them to drink from wells of their own choosing. Once while visiting a church school, the students complained that though the teacher was encouraging, she was afraid to let them do their own projects. The teacher had used a lot of film in her class, but when the students wanted to do an independent film for their closing project, the teacher did not think it was a good idea. Education is a reciprocal affair that creates a back-and-forth movement between the teacher and the student. Too often much of our teaching in church ends on Sunday, without any follow-up during the week. We talk about compassion and love without giving students the opportunity to share how they have experienced trying to live compassionate and loving lives. The more students and teachers share about how their faith gets lived out on a daily basis, the more authentic will be their religious commitments. Sharing provides a relationship of knowledge and trust that grows and informs the experience of the teacher and the student in their family, school, and church life. This interchange enables a relationship of knowledge and trust. Through it the student learns from the religious teacher the ways to engage family, school, church, and society.

Education is really about conversation that covers personal experience and how they intersect with the God whom we know as Creator, Redeemer, and Sanctifier. These conversations require the exchange of ideas about ourselves and God, the questions we have about life, and our discussions about social issues. Conversation involves an equal exchange of listening, questioning, and responding. Our goal is not necessarily to answer the questions or come to conclusions, but to find ways of turning our sharing into life-changing moments. For instance, how do teachers talk about death, love, money, immigrants, poor people, and sex? Those are life issues that are not often enough discussed in church.

Conversation is the best curriculum. When churches and educators in the church dedicate time to having conversation about God, we set the stage for conversion and education that is liberating and effective. Spontaneous conversation holds a special place in education, even though at times planned conversation is needed.

Conversations help to evaluate and redirect the course of the educational process. Again, it is important to recognize that our agenda must always be held lightly and open to the Spirit. Because education is a drawing out of what is inside the individual, it is unlikely that a preplanned curriculum will best serve the needs of a group. One church-school teacher invented a game called "Topics from a Hat." She wrote topics gleaned from current events, news, and the movies on slips of paper and placed them in a hat. Choosing topics at random, she asked her students what Jesus would do and what they would do. There were topics about leaving one's friend on the highway to go for help, taking money from an abandoned house, cheating on tests, the use of money, and Christian service. No one enters into a conversation and expects to do all the talking. The *sharing* of information needs to be honored, and those who listen need ways to honor what they hear. Education involves more than the formation of the other person; it requires that the one who is educating is open to formation in the process. Do Christian educators ever think of themselves as being "formed in the habits" of the faith they profess?

It is important that the educator bears in mind that she or he has one mouth and two ears. The lessons being taught are just as important for the educator.

Once again you are invited to spend some time with the definitions and thoughts that I have shared on education. What would you add? What would you subtract? How would you define education? How has God educated you? How have you been educated by life? What is the most exciting, reciprocal, and dynamic educational experience you have had? What roles do wisdom and education play in your life?

Take some time to pray for the gift of wisdom, perhaps using the following prayer:

Loving God, you know that I often do not know what to do or say. Give me wisdom so that what I do and say may reflect your wisdom and love. Let your wisdom inspire me so that I may love you with all my heart, mind, and soul. Through your wisdom, let me see you in all my brothers and sisters, especially those whom I teach. Amen.

I invite you to pay special attention to what happens as you pray for wisdom. Here is a story that illustrates an approach in wisdom:

Kathleen always prepared her lessons well for class. She prided herself on being a good teacher, and she loved her students. But she had one big problem that she could not figure out how to solve. In every class she would ask her students a question. As she lectured she could tell who had done the homework. She made sure that she always called on those who did not do the homework. Naturally, she never got the answers she wanted. "Who said this?" "What is the meaning of this?" Even though she did the same thing to the same students every day, she was surprised that it did not make them study and get the answers prepared for her. One day she had a teaching assistant teach her class, and for the first time, she decided to stay in the back of the classroom, without the students noticing. When the teaching assistant finished his lesson, he had fifteen minutes remaining. "Who would like to tell me what you think about today's lessons?" he asked. Kathleen was shocked to discover that the students who had never spoken before were the ones most engaged in the discussion.

As we think about education in different contexts, reflect on our experience with education, and continue our education ministry, I hope we will come to recognize more deeply how education, done as conversation, informs everything. Teaching by conversation is not limited to words, because our actions quite frequently speak more loudly.

Because God called us out of the earth, we have an innate need to call out and respond in kind. The fact that we are created, and Christians believe that God created all things, is a clear sign that all people and things are educated, in need of education, and able to educate.

When God spoke, something happened: Let there be light, and there was light. The Scriptures give us no indication of how long it took for light to appear, but appear it did. A parent imitates God in a similar fashion by saying to the toddler, "Give this to Papa." The child takes the plate, hesitates, examines it, hesitates again, then haltingly walks over and hands Papa the plate. The mother and father applaud. What would our children and students look like if we had the patience of God? What would our education process look like if we taught about God, faith, and love, and waited attentively for what we say to have an effect on them? In creation God calls out light, animals, trees, and humans, and then affirms that they are good. Speaking, waiting for a response, and affirming are habits that we can learn from God, who created us.

Education can be formal or informal, but it is a necessity of life. In our discussion I have linked education to the very act of creation, and I want to close this section on education by suggesting that we come to value education as intrinsic to humanity.

We need one another, because only in relationship with one another are we led to recognize this truth that is common to all God's children.

3 Teachers Teaching with a Mission

Introductory Meditations

We have discussed and meditated on education, seeking to foster a renewed vision of education and our roles as educators, as well as a desire to grow as better educators.
- What in this section on education have you found most useful?
- Which elements of this section provide materials for prayer?

Before we go on to discuss the teaching process, let us pause for a while and do some reflection. Ask yourself:
- When have I found a teacher to be exciting?
- Which teacher helped me see that education was reciprocal?
- What have I found most dynamic in my experience as a student?

Set aside some time to examine the questions. Reflect on them and write down your thoughts and feelings. Finally, return to the preceding story about Kathleen's class method.
- What do you think Kathleen learned?
- What are the moments when you feel most disconnected from your students?
- What excites you about teaching? What bores you?
- Who are the students you ignore or pay the most attention to, and why?

Teachers Teaching with a Mission
Teaching and Teachers

A saying in Proverbs 29:18 states that without a vision, the people perish. Without a mission, religious education will likewise perish. Christian education comes out of a vocation from God. When God created humans, the charge was given to be fruitful and multiply. This charge is about more than mere procreation; it is a challenge to pass on the experience of God through building communities of sharing and conversation.

Teachers claim their identity by understanding themselves as being called by God to teach. In their teaching they share who God is and how God acts in humanity and in individual hearts. Obviously their ability to share depends a lot on their lived experience of God. A mathematics teacher need not think about mathematics the whole day, but a religious teacher always has her relationship with God in view. All her life is informed by faith, and she lives knowing that she has a mission from God. It is out of this conscious living that she teaches. When teachers accept that they are called by God, they find comfort in knowing that God will provide the graces they need to carry out their ministry of teaching.

The mission of teachers is to talk about God's activities in the world, to study the Bible, to be transformed by the Bible, and to show ways in which the Bible and the Christian life bring decisive action to bear on the events of our lives. In creation God teaches us much about who God is and how God acts.

I believe that in the story of creation, one aspect of God that we discover is God as teacher. Through creation it is as though God teaches the created things to be the best they can be. God's intent for each created thing is that it lives into the most perfect existence of what it is.

I believe that creation is most aptly described as God the teacher, creating and teaching humans to be creators, students, and teachers. That is why one of God's first commands is for creation to be fruitful and multiply. We are called to be cocreators. Through creation and the Incarnation, we see God at work. God calls us to be not only creators but also people who *incarnate* the divine presence.

Because we are followers of God, we see our call to teach as having the mission of creating anew and incarnating God's world today. God did not go elsewhere to begin creation, but instead entered into the formlessness and void that the world had to offer. From this God educated, or drew out, light and all that followed from the darkness and confusion. For teachers today no other landscape exists in which we can work except to engage in the messiness of human life and seek to bring light and productivity from it. This is what we set out to do when we teach informed by our faith.

Put simply, creation is God's best way of teaching humans. In Psalm 19:1–4, we read: "The heavens are telling the glory of God; and the firmament proclaims his handiwork. Day to day pours forth speech, and night to night declares knowledge. There is no speech, nor are there words; their voice is not heard; yet their voice goes out through all the earth, and their words to the end of the world."

For Reflection:
• How does nature teach you about God?
• How does God as Creator influence how you live and teach?
• How do you teach without words?

Teaching is the challenge that the Christian community faces in reclaiming its mission. Those with a good knowledge of human experience or the Bible will recognize that life is about humans and God learning together.

One lesson of creation is that all things have an origin; we believe they originate in and from God. People today want to know what God has to do with their lives and how to connect to God's plan for their lives. Of course, most people do not express their desires this way. But I believe that there is a search for understanding what role the spiritual and the Spirit play in the lives of the ordinary person. This is one of the reasons people attend church. Unfortunately we do not provide people with an adequate or useful understanding of their relationship to God. We fail by not giving people sufficient opportunity to raise their questions about God.

Christians stand in relationship with the Creator, ready to listen, learn, and discover the truths of existence. God is the ultimate teacher, and we are all students. But even as we all stand as students before God, we are all given the tasks of teaching our experience of God. In teaching our experience of God, we set out on the path of fulfilling our mission.

Another way of understanding God's act of teaching is to examine the interplay of silence, the spoken word, and action. Our creation stories in the first chapters of Genesis show the silence of God, the voice of God, and the activity of God that causes the creation of the world. God's silence, God's words, and God's actions form the methodology of the teaching ministry. As teachers get excited about the teaching ministry as mission, they will experience a growing sense of the importance of silence, a meditative silence that informs both the words and actions of the lessons.

While I was visiting a church school, a young man told me that he had problems teaching the class. The children are too hyper, he told me. By the time they settle down, he continued, it is time for them to go. I asked him to tell me how he began each session. Apparently he began each class with rousing choruses, and encouraged the children to sing and dance. That was his way of trying to make the class time exciting. I asked him if I could visit his class for the next three weeks.

On my second visit, I understood why this eager young man was having problems. True, the children loved being there in class with him. The lively choruses made them happy and excited, but that was the problem. It was not so much that the students were hyper, but that he was making them hyper. He got them so excited that they needed another fifteen minutes to settle down. He wanted to teach during the time the children were still excited. By the third visit and after talking to him during the week, we came upon a new idea.

We decided to begin each class with three minutes of silence, then two minutes of simple guided meditations. I led the first session with the children. We lit a candle, turned down the lights, and invited the children to sit quietly, focus on the light, and be aware of their breathing. There were many giggles in the first session, but soon the children got into it. After the five minutes were up, the teacher gave the lesson. But before he dismissed the class, I invited them to sing a lively chorus. Using singing as the last activity had the effect of getting them excited as they left the class and probably making them more likely to talk about their experience in church school.

When we understand the role of silence as part of our mission of teaching, we likewise better understand the potential of words. In our busy lives, we do not have much room for quiet ,and although God is described as "the Word," silence is just as characteristic of God. Creation comes out of silence. It is as though silence were the supreme companion of God. From the Genesis story, we get a sense that there was nonverbal communication—what I am calling silence—up to the point of creation. It is out of the silence that God commenced the acts of creation, starting with light.

We often miss the importance of the creation stories in Genesis. Those stories point to an order that God creates, an order in which we are invited to participate by in turn ordering our actions. God's actions increase with each passing "day," and so we are invited as cocreators to grow in our determination to make the world a better place. Another element in the creation story is the element of rest, or Sabbath. God rests, and that is just as important as his acts of creating. Everything in the creation story completes everything else. Because we have much to learn from an attentive reading of the creation story, I invite you to spend some time reading the passage from Genesis and see what comes up for you in regard to your teaching ministry.

The whole of creation, every human person, everything that lives—seen and unseen—forms part of the divine lesson plan. God's involvement in creation shows us how we are called to participate in the very mission of God.

Our existence in this created world, from which we get all our experiences, is our greatest teacher. The starting point of creation's lesson is love. We believe that God created us out of love and teaches us to love God and one another. God teaches us to love, and we are called to teach love. Put simply, our mission as teachers resides in our ability to be agents of love.

Now let us take another historical trip to gain an overview of the role of teachers in the past. By examining what went before us, we can compare our present-day methodologies and see if we can sharpen our skills as teachers.

A Brief Historical View of Teachers
Greek Teachers

Socrates distinguishes himself as one of the premiere Greek teachers by his use of questions to arrive at deeper knowledge. He leads his students to an acknowledgement that they know *nothing.* In debates about the meaning of life or in scientific debates, he leads his listeners to talk about various subjects with the goal of having them realize that they do not know as much as they thought they did. By constantly questioning his students, he leads them to a deeper search for and love of knowledge. Greek teachers were lovers of knowledge, on a mission to pursue knowledge. How would you describe yourself as a teacher? Do you see yourself as seeking out new ways to teach and to learn about what you teach? We might better understand and grow in our roles as religious teachers if we see our mission as being to pass on to our students our love of knowledge.

Teachers must love knowledge. But what does it mean to love knowledge? I believe that to love knowledge, we must walk around with questions in our heart. These questions help us to keep seeking the truth. It is said that life is not about answering questions, but questioning answers. When we seek to question all the answers we have heard, we grow in knowledge. What is *love* that we can use it to describe a relationship with knowledge?

To teach requires that we ask questions. Unfortunately, many of us believe that in order to teach, we need to say things over and over again. Many times we do not leave opportunities for our students to question us. Maybe this stems from our unwillingness to question ourselves. But questions can be the most effective way to breathe new life into a discussion or the best way to introduce a new topic.

Jesus also asked many questions as a way of introducing his teaching. His questions pose challenges, clarify, give contrasts, rebuke, and help his listeners to think of things in new ways. Jesus knew that questions have the ability to provoke an audience to think of God and their human interactions in a new way. Keep in mind that if we are imitators of Christ in our teaching, the "Socratic method" of teaching might well be a good way to teach. Good questions educate best because they draw the answers out of the students.

Look at this passage of Scripture, and see how Jesus teaches:

> Then the Pharisees went and plotted to entrap him in what he said. So they sent their disciples to him, along with the Herodians, saying, "Teacher, we know that you are sincere, and teach the way of God in accordance with truth, and show deference to no one; for you do not regard people with partiality. Tell us, then, what you think. Is it lawful to pay taxes to the emperor, or not?" But Jesus, aware of their malice, said, "Why are you putting me to the test, you hypocrites? Show me the coin used for the tax." And they brought him a denarius. Then he said to them, "Whose head is this, and whose title?" They answered, "The emperor's." Then he said to them, "Give therefore to the emperor the things that are the emperor's, and to God the things that are God's." (Matthew 22:15–21)

- Close your eyes and imagine that you are the people who are asking Jesus this question. Notice the expression on Jesus' face when you ask the question.
- Now try to remember a moment when a student or a child asked you a question. Recall your answer.
- Briefly repeat this meditation, and see if you can think of a question that you could ask that might help the student or child answer the question for herself or himself.

One of the best ways of using this method of asking questions is to anticipate further possible questions. You might start by making a list of ten possible questions for every lesson you prepare. Be gentle with yourself as you make these questions, and be prepared to be surprised. The ultimate goal of preparing questions is to ready yourself for whatever may happen in the classroom. Keep in mind that every question has value. The manner in which you welcome the questions will determine how involved your students get in the lessons. There will always be more questions than answers, and the sooner you accept that the better.

Loving knowledge is to embrace it in a committed relationship. All that we know and hope to teach needs to remain open to questions that we or others may pose. This process is similar to being in a relationship. When we are in love, we ask questions and open ourselves to being asked questions. Like the love we feel for another human being, there is no way to capture fully or in one moment the essence of the person; likewise, love of knowledge is a lifelong process of loving.

Knowledge, love, and the human person intersect in every teaching moment. It is as though our answered and unanswered questions lead us into a deeper knowledge of who we are in relationship to others. Great teachers always teach us to love our questions, to love ourselves, to love others, and to love knowledge. This is why the Greeks defined the teacher as one who loves knowledge and wisdom, *the philosopher.*

Teachers, then, are seekers of knowledge, wisdom, truth, and love. They commit themselves to this search, and because of their love of humanity, they share what they discover and listen to what others have discovered.

The teacher is one who spends time engaged in linking the heavens and the earth, showing the separation and the connection between the spiritual and the material.

Teachers organized the Greek society to reflect the place of the gods, their interaction with humanity, and how a love for truth and beauty could bring peace and enlightenment. For many Greek philosophers, teaching involved a journey of engaging fundamental questions. For the Greeks, nothing was too sacred to be questioned as a means of teaching.

I have touched only briefly on the Greek view of the teacher and teaching. In summary, the Greeks felt that the teacher had a most important role in society: The teacher was known primarily for his love of knowledge, and therefore it was the teacher's responsibility to pass on the love of learning to the rest of society. In today's society, parents, teachers, and other adults share the important role of ensuring that students develop a love for knowledge. In the church we are responsible for creating communities of seekers, communities informed by their love of the faith.

African Teachers
The ancient African communities gave special prominence to the teacher. Africans understood teachers as representative of the spirit in all created things. All things could teach, and human beings were bound to learn the correct posture before all created things.

Created things reflected the order and the disorder of the universe. Animals could speak, trees could move, spirits could possess objects, humans could change forms, and the gods could be anywhere. Therefore all of nature was to be respected, and humans had to know their place in the order of things. All this provided sufficient material for the African teacher.

Unlike the Greek Socratic methods, Africans did not believe that one should question certain elders, priests, royal family members, or aspects of reality. An African proverb reminds us that "what you don't know is bigger than you." Teachers are entrusted with the task of teaching respect for mysteries and the big things in life.

Human beings in ancient Africa had to learn which questions and answers they could live without knowing. Teachers taught humility and respect and warned against those who tried to outwit the gods and the spirits.

A good teacher also had to create in the student a *love* for the story. Hence much of the ancient African custom centered on the community sitting around at night listening to stories. For the African the story told by a good teacher took on new life, became embodied, became flesh. A storyteller would often begin by saying, "My story breaks sharply; don't let it break its arms, don't let it break its head."

Stories were not made to fall on the ground, but to be eaten by the student. When the student eats a story and takes it home, the story transforms the student and eventually the whole community. Teachers mainly taught at night, so that the quiet and the darkness would influence the sleep of the student, causing him or her to die with the words and wake the next day with a new life.

African teachers appeared in many forms. The king, the shaman, the medicine man, the elder, and the diviner all helped to show Africans their relationship with reality.

In many African societies, love of knowledge was manifested in one's engagement with the family, the earth, the spirits, and the gods. More than the question, it was the story that was the medium for the teacher. Within the story the teacher could break the rules by having the characters ask the dangerous questions. The audience learned from the outcome of that action.

Stories were told about kings, spirits, tricksters, farmers, masters, and servants. Together, the stories treated all the themes and events of life. The stories were oral, and almost never written down. The power of the teacher's use of words was the elusive nature of words. These stories had the power for *catharsis,* in the same way the Greek, Hebrew, and Shakespearean tragedies help to broaden the moral experience of the student or audience.

In this same way, questions help unearth a new love of knowledge and learning in students today. Allowing students to tell their stories can unlock powerful tools for learning. How we help our students tell their stories determines how much they open themselves to the stories of the faith we wish to pass on to them. What a difference it makes in our churches when we invite students to tell their stories of feeling loved before we begin to tell them about God's love. Telling personal stories can serve the purpose of questions, because to tell a story is to answer the question "What similar thing has happened to you?"

For the African the teacher was one who lived the stories by treasuring them and sharing their riches. Society depended on mutual teaching, on the process of passing on stories, each person teaching the other how to respect the different stations and mysteries in life.

Jewish Teachers

The ancient Jewish people had a rich and elaborate history of teaching and teachers. Both the oral and the written traditions figured into their understanding of the teaching process and the teacher. Most well-respected teachers did not write down their thoughts, but because of the teacher's wisdom and fame, their disciples did.

Here again we see a unique requirement for the Jewish people: the teacher was viewed as anointed by God and speaking for God to the community. Teachers exercised their duty out of a belief that God created the world and the moral order, and that God had called the Jews to be the chosen people.

Teachers in the Jewish tradition pointed the way to God and the Torah. A teacher mirrored the wisdom of God revealed in the Torah. Rabbis pointed to the important role of the Torah in the life of the Jewish community.

Right living, right relationships, and righteousness were the main lessons taught by teachers. Here wisdom is linked with holiness. The teacher was not one who pursued knowledge for knowledge's sake but one who pursued knowledge of God as a means of being holy. A teacher believed that his role was to help sanctify the community and to lead the community to God. Thus teaching became linked to holiness and prophecy, because prophets taught the wishes of God for the community.

In addition to the prophets and judges, Jews had a special place for those considered to be *wise men,* especially during the reign of Solomon. These men founded schools to prepare students morally and politically for the business, religious, political, and diplomatic worlds. They became famous for their teachings, in which they commonly used poetry and proverbs as a means of sharing knowledge.

Like the storyteller in the African tradition, the wise men were recognized as spiritual community leaders, along with the prophets and priests. These wise men had much in common with the philosophers of Greek culture, too. They operated from a rational and experimental premise, which often led to conflict with the religious and political leaders.

Still, they were highly respected as teachers. What is important about these wise men is that they help us remember that ways of teaching are as numerous as the stars in the sky.

For the Jews who lived their lives closely linked to the Torah, there was a strong belief in the need for the nation to listen to prophets as well. Moses was seen as a point of reference, and in many ways the teacher strove to imitate Moses: the one who had encountered God, seen the face of God, led the people out of bondage, and acted as mediator between God and human beings.

Because of the role of the Torah in the lives of Jews, especially the command for each Jew to read it, obey it, dialogue with it, and find life in it, Jews also readily accepted the possibility that everyone is a teacher. Thus in many ways, whoever paid attention to the Torah, dialogued with it, interpreted it, and offered it as life for the nation could be considered a teacher, or rabbi.

For the Jews, a true teacher could not change the essential message of the Torah or offer something outside the Torah. A true teacher was one who believed in the primary position of the Torah, its ability to bring the community together and to God. Teachers mirrored the Torah by using stories, poetry, and various methods to talk about their experience of God.

Asian Teachers

In the Asian tradition, teachers played a significant role in the formation of society. Called master, guru, sensei or "the enlightened one," these teachers led lives of high repute and distinguished themselves by strict adherence to ethical living.

The Asian culture placed great emphasis on integrity, so a teacher in this tradition lived a holy life. Few teachers recruited students; for the most part, a teacher's fame would spread by word of mouth and students might travel a great distance to study with a renowned teacher.

Confucius, who lived about four hundred years before Christ, is one of the most influential philosophers and thinkers in the history of the world. His teaching emphasizes a philosophy that is ethical and practical. He believed that the individual and society would be better if people focused on the five virtues of kindness, uprightness, decorum, wisdom, and faithfulness.

Confucius believed that people learn morality best by keeping the values of society ever in their mind. For this reason, he taught by using maxims. If a citizen could recite the golden rule—do unto others as you would like them to do to you—and keep it in mind, he or she would be less likely to harm another person.

And so Confucius, and many of the teachers who followed him, believed that a moral life is to be achieved by studying the wisdom of the ancestors, observing the rituals of the culture, and imitating the lives of holy men and women. He believed and instilled in his students that it was useless to preach without practicing what one preached, and that it was useless to study if one did not intend to put what one had learned into practice. Confucius stands as the supreme teacher from Asia because of his commitment to the good of the individual and his positive outlook that everyone was capable of moral living.

In the Hindu tradition, the teacher is called a guru. The role of the guru is to lead the disciples to spiritual and emotional liberation. Gurus insist that the disciple remain faithful to what is prescribed for spiritual growth: fasting, recitation of mantras, and religious disciplines.

As in other traditions, much emphasis was placed on spending time with the teacher. Gurus often used stories to teach about morality and the path to enlightenment. Many gurus would not allow their words to be written down, insisting instead that students pay close attention to their words so as to learn and remember. They also insisted on absolute respect for their words and complete reverence in their presence. Sometimes the teacher or guru was considered to be the incarnation of a god.

Teachers of martial arts espouse that practice brings about perfection. These teachers have a special place in the Asian tradition because they, more than any other teacher, highlight the role of the body in ethical living. By teaching the art of self-defense they instill a discipline of anticipating the reactions and actions of the "other." Though some have taught martial arts as a means of lording it over others, many forms of this art insist that students practice humility and gentleness.

Asian teachers represent a methodology that focuses on the teacher as a means to achieve a greater connection to the community. Teachers in this tradition insist that rules be strictly followed, and physical punishment can be used to reinforce the rules of the community. The overall emphasis is the restoration of order in the life of the individual and society, and the integration of body, mind, and soul.

4 Contemporary Attitudes about Teaching

Introductory Meditations

Before we continue our discussion on teachers and teaching, I invite you to spend some time thinking about what you have just read.

Read Matthew 5:1–11. Imagine that you are one of the people listening to Jesus. Situate yourself close to the disciples, and see if you can notice how the crowds are reacting to Jesus.

Now ask yourself the following questions:
• How does Jesus teach?
• What does Jesus teach?
• In what ways do I think Jesus is a good teacher?
• How does Jesus' teaching affect my life?
• How do I witness to or teach the Jesus story?

Spend at least fifteen minutes with these questions, and once again take time to write or draw the results of your meditation.

One day a mother said to her daughter, Kathleen, "You should go to church school."

"I do not want to go, because the children do not like me and I do not like them."

"You must go," insisted the mother.

"I do not want to go, but if you give me three reasons, I will think about it."

"It is Sunday and you should go, I am your mother and I am telling you to go, and finally, you are the church-school teacher."

Contemporary Attitudes about Teaching

A few statements about teaching and teachers:
- Teaching does not make a teacher rich.
- Teaching is a pastoral ministry.
- Teaching presupposes interest in the life of the students.
- There can only be one teacher in a classroom.
- People from broken homes make poor teachers.
- God is the only teacher.
- Elderly people make poor teachers.
- Teachers are fingers pointing to the moon.
- A teacher is fun.
- The young have nothing to teach and are also poor teachers.
- Teachers are lovers.
- Teachers are lovers of life.
- A teacher is one who causes chaos.
- A teacher is a healer.
- Teachers are revolutionaries.
- A teacher builds community.
- Teachers can only teach what they know.
- A teacher has moral authority.
- A teacher is the moral authority.
- Teachers are professional.
- Teachers are good storytellers.
- The government has not made teachers a priority.
- The church has not made teachers a priority.
- I am a good teacher.

I invite you to spend time with these positions, attitudes, and definitions. I have been collecting responses from around the world. What would you add to the list? What would you subtract?

Mark your five favorite definitions. Mark the statements you disagree with or do not like. Take some time to reflect on and pray about your responses. You can always come back to this section. As you already know, what you think in your heart will influence how you teach or are taught.

Teaching is defined formally as the act or process of giving systematic information to a person about a subject. Notice the phrase *process of giving.* Present-day understanding of the process of giving is that a gift is a free offering, and that the one who receives it has the onus to reject or accept it. For our purpose here, I see the act of teaching as an act of giving. It involves enabling a person, by instruction and training, to do something, especially because teaching normally emphasizes principles for living.

Another meaning that connects teaching to education is one that defines teaching as *inducing* a person by example or punishment to do or not do a thing. Teaching is also synonymous with doctrine, or whatever is taught. I prefer the word *giving,* and will summarize this definition of teaching and teachers by saying that teaching is a process of imparting a gift.

Much of our discussion has focused on the concept of *gift.* As Christians we believe that all things come from God as gifts; indeed, our very existence is God's gift to us. From that understanding, then all that we do and are to each other is gift.

Teaching and the ministry of teaching are gifts from God. As teachers, as those who practice teaching, we share in the divine work of God by encouraging wisdom, giving of our knowledge, and sharing our lives with others. As Christians our interconnectedness demands of us that we share our lives with others.

Today's teachers must give of their lives, much more than giving theories and tradition. I cannot stress enough the need for teachers to know themselves, to know the inner atmosphere of their hearts, and to integrate their experience with the lived experience of God. Only when teachers, particularly in the church, live from this principle does teaching become, in the words of *The Book of Common Prayer*, "The Gifts of God for the People of God" (364).

Because God's gifts are free, our teaching process fosters a communal relationship with God that honors the view that all are freely taught and gifted by God. Teachers have the task of pointing out to students the wisdom and gifts of God. Students do not lack the gifts and wisdom of God, but are at a different stage on their journey of discovering them.

Those who teach best are those who can say, "I have been

there," or "I am there." This requires great self-knowledge on the part of the one who is teaching, who must also know when to share his or her life and when to allow the student to come to a decision or solution on his or her own.

Teaching reaffirms the human experience and the giftedness of belonging and responsibility. In short, teaching is a way of making clear how we belong and why we are responsible to one another. To belong and to be responsible is to claim the gifts of God. Claiming these gifts allows Christians to accept the dual roles of disciple and rabbi.

Teaching, then, fosters in all of us the ability to get in touch with our giftedness as prophets of God, whatever our life stage may be. Those who teach are charged with the responsibility of calling students to recognize that they are made in the image and likeness of God, which is to say that they are sharers in God's wisdom and mystery.

Christian teachers help the church community to understand what it means to be wise and what it means to be curious about mystery. So much of life is mystery, and teaching is a means of learning how to encounter the mystery. Like Moses, we must learn how to take off our shoes. Like the disciples, we need to learn how to sit at the feet of Jesus or to sit on the mountain and listen to him.

• *How have you experienced teaching and learning as a gift?*
• *How is your learning style different as an adult when compared to your childhood?*
• *How do you approach mystery?*

Teaching in Brazil

Years ago, I had the opportunity to teach in Brazil. I had degrees in philosophy, theology, and literature, but nothing prepared me for the ways in which I would learn from many Brazilians who had not had any formal education.

Earlier I spoke about the importance of seeing each member in the community as teacher and as student, and I also mentioned that the professionally trained can learn plenty from those who have not had much formal education, and vice versa.

This understanding reflects a teaching method that I encountered among certain people of Brazil who lived on the margins of society. Cherishing the gifts of their faith, especially the Bible, they wanted to ensure that the gifts of faith and knowledge of the Bible were passed on to their children. So they made it a priority to get together to talk about their faith, the Bible, and their lives. Though they were marginalized, these people embraced their faith with a passion not often seen in North American parishes.

Without having much formal education, they knew the importance of knowledge. All their lives they had survived on the knowledge that had been passed down to them by their parents through stories, prayer, and work in the fields. Few technological tools gave more accurate predictions of the weather than did these farmers. Like their acquired knowledge of nature, they made a commitment to educate and teach themselves about the Bible, their faith, and the country.

They formed themselves into "base communities," and decided to study the Bible. They came up with three steps for their teaching method. The first was to see or hear (*ver, ouvir,*) the second was to judge (*julgar,*) and the third was to act (*agir.*) The coordinator or teacher of the group would be a woman or a man who believed in the teaching method, could facilitate the discussions in the room, and could enable each person to have a voice (*voz, vez*) and time to express themselves.

I have never witnessed a more progressive teaching strategy. Nothing was ever taken as a given, everything was open to discussion, and each person in the group had a right to share, question, and teach. When they wanted to teach the Bible, they read it one or two times and discussed it, and each person's opinion was valued because each person was seen as a teacher.

This was their process of judging: they judged by giving their opinions and thoughts. They judged by claiming the dignity to decide what was best for their community. In the Bible they clung to clues and stories that showed that God wanted them to have a life of quality and freedom. And so they devoted their time to comparing their life experience with what they understood as God's desire for their life. Their experience of life gave them the authority to judge. After they shared their teachings with one another, it was time to act on what they had learned.

Living out what they had learned came from the group's sharing. They talked and shared, listened to one another, and *led* the meaningful actions out of one another. At the end of the meetings, each person was fully aware of where the community wanted to go. All were well taught because all were involved, and all could respect the teaching and the teacher in the other.

Another aspect of my experience of teaching in Brazil was the liberative aspect of teaching: teaching for liberation. Teachers were those who had struggled with oppression, not alone but within the context of the community. What teachers in the base communities did was to teach from their experience of liberation.

Teaching, therefore, was not only a spiritual activity but also a political one. Like Moses, these teachers believed that they had received a mandate from God to free the people. So like Moses, religious teachers in Brazil teach that God has seen their oppression and wants to set them free.

Colonization and its effects, the history of loss and displacement, the ills of racism, and structural poverty form the core of the lessons taught. All this information is shared through reflection and discussion, and is done within the context of realizing that they are God's people and God wants them to be free.

In these situations of oppression, teachers live with their students, march with their students, work with their students, and die with their students. The whole community teaches the effects of colonization and oppression, and learns together how to work for freedom.

For these teachers and students the teaching process is tantamount to experiencing life. Like Martin Luther King Jr., these teachers "talk the talk and walk the walk." Teaching in this context then becomes a celebration and an anticipation of freedom: to teach is to impart knowledge of the utopia. Teaching stands as the surest means for emancipation from mental and physical oppression.

Brazilian teachers in the base communities, I believe, best illustrate the unity of teaching, in that their teaching embraces all of life, the religious and the political—the religious as political, and the political as religious. To teach is to create in the minds and hearts of those who are listening a strong desire to know *reality*. Life with all its glories, possibilities, and suffering is looked at from the side of those who are oppressed, allowing them to embrace the goodness in stark contrast to the evils, and to dedicate their lives to changing the systems of oppression.

How many schools and churches in North America ignore the oppression of African Americans, women, gays, lesbians, poor people, unemployed people, and non-Christians? If God's message to Moses was to go and teach liberation, how can we do justice to God's call if we do not teach the evils of an affluent, materialistic, racist, sexist, and oppressive society?

Of course, the United States has its prophetic voices, but religious teaching and instruction become deceitful when they join in pretending that evil, suffering, pain, and poverty do not exist.

Teachers point to the community and the world, the church and the city, the individual and the society. In so doing, teaching becomes a means of helping students and teachers ask the question, "Who is my neighbor?" So, for example, teachers must help those who are affluent to realize that people are dying because of poverty right in their own communities, rather than pointing only to the suffering and poverty beyond American shores. What this does is keep us in the dark about our complicity in the suffering of others and also engage us in denial of the poverty within the United States.

To teach solely about God's love and mercy without paying attention to the Christian teachings about justice and care for the poor is to do an injustice. Those who teach will teach best by helping children, youth, and adults to know that there are children, youth, and adults elsewhere in the country dying of hunger, dying before their time. We are connected to one another because God is the Creator of all of us. To teach the image of God to students, to teach life and the meaning of life is to teach that in our freedom we oftentimes desecrate the image of God and cause death. As we teach the meaning of life in a society that promotes individual rights, we need to explore ways of teaching about the importance of community and caring for others.

Like the Greek, African, Jewish, and Asian teachers described earlier, teachers today can capture the communal importance of education. By this I mean that teaching can be seen as a means of structuring the community, creating prophets who denounce oppression, creating the space to question societal myths that perpetuate the masking of reality.

Christian teachers often prefer to limit their purview to the joy of the Resurrection, God's love for us, and whatever else feels comfortable. But there is a crying need to teach against the status quo, because Christianity is not about comfort. I hope that in our teaching we can discover ways to lead students beyond the comfort of their sheltered experiences into those of others. One such way is to use mission trips throughout our parishes. Exposing members of the parishes to different cultures, life experiences, and social classes within the United States leads to a more realistic view of life and a more compassionate posture toward others.

If our Christian education is always a gift, then we are called to be gifts for others. As imitators of Jesus, we grow in the recognition that Jesus spent much of his life serving others. We are therefore called to be a community for others. Christian teaching has to concentrate on the truth that we are the gifts of God for the people of God, and on these questions: Why am I a gift? Why do others need me as a gift? What is the gift they most need?

These questions need to form the base of any Christian teaching. In them we encounter the presence of the living God. As gifts we must concern ourselves with the oppression of others, and devote our lives not to our own personal aggrandizement but to the needs of the poor, the stranger, the suffering, the hungry, and the weak.

God comes not only for the individual student or classroom but for all people, those we see and those we do not see. Teachers must help students question their reality, their stories, the Bible, society, and the myths of the American dream.

Teaching within this paradigm best reflects the countercultural nature of the life, mission, and teachings of Jesus the rabbi, our truest teacher. Jesus as teacher was divine, human, spiritual, political, local, and cosmic. To teach as a religious mission or ministry is to teach the Jesus who challenged the status quo, encouraged liberation, celebrated the gifts of God, helped others, and gave his life because of his faith in God. Can we teach Jesus without imitating him?

5 Imitators of God

Introductory Meditations

Before I go on to share a few thoughts on teaching, formation, and education as acts of imitating God, let us pause to meditate on Matthew 25:31–46.

I invite you to read this passage again slowly, then put the Bible down and go do something else. Make a conscious effort to think about what Jesus said. Sometime later in the day, return to the passage and read it again.

Ask yourself the following questions:
- What is Jesus teaching?
- Why does Jesus want me to think of the hungry, the imprisoned, the thirsty, and the stranger?
- When I teach do I ever mention these people?
- If I were the judge of the world, how would I judge in light of this passage?

Do take time with the passage and the questions. Write down your thoughts or share them with someone. You may want to make a list of the realities for people in a poor section of your city or make a list of some of the issues that are never mentioned in your church or church school.

A parish search committee chose the son of the deceased rector to be the new rector. They thought: He will be good because he is the son of our beloved rector. After a few months, they began complaining. The new priest allowed children to participate in the liturgies, got rid of evening prayer, preached about politics, and started adult education in the parish. People in the parish complained to the bishop, and asked the rector why he was so unlike his father. The new rector replied: "I am quite like my father. You see I am imitating his best trait: he never imitated anyone. He was himself and he taught me to do things my way"

(adapted from a story told to me by Tony de Mello in 1986).

Give ear, O my people, to my teaching;
Incline your ears to the words of my mouth.
I will open my mouth in a parable;
I will speak dark sayings from of old,
things that we have heard and known,
that our fathers have told us.
We will not hide them from our children
but teach the coming generation.
(Adapted from Psalm 78:1-4)

Respond to the following questions:
•What does it mean to imitate God?
•How do I imitate God in my daily life?
•Are my attempts to love and teach imitations of God?
•What quality or aspect of my life would I like my students to imitate?

Take a few moments to reflect on God as teacher and ask yourself what it is that you would like to learn from God. Then make a list of five things that you would like to begin teaching or continue teaching about God.

Imitators of God
Imitating God

> If then there is any encouragement in Christ, any consolation
> from love, any sharing in the Spirit, any compassion and sympa-
> thy, make my joy complete: be of the same mind, having the same
> love, being in full accord and of one mind. (Philippians 2:1–2)

Teachers share in the educational process of God, teaching
the world the ways of God. Teachers find themselves in a unique
position because they are faced with the mandate of living what
they teach. As with all Christians, Christian teachers receive a call
to strive to live the message they teach and proclaim.

Proclamation of the joys of the kingdom, the righteousness
of the kingdom, and the justice of God's reign soon becomes scan-
dalous on the lips of a teacher who does not proclaim in her or his
life the joy, holiness, right living, and justice of following God. The
demand on the Christian teacher to practice and love what she or
he teaches can lead to an integrated ministry of teaching.

A relationship of intimacy needs to exist between the
teacher's life and what is taught, especially if the teacher teaches
the values of Christian living. All that we teach about Jesus—the
messages of love, grace, self-giving, the inclusive kingdom—should
be manifested in the life of the teacher, the students, the church,
and the world. The message of and about Jesus can help us integrate our experiences of suffering, hope, grace, life, and death.

Teaching Jesus requires that we teach life and the courage to
live. In the teacher students must see a commitment to church
and society and learn Christian responses to the issues that arise
in the church and society. If teachers are cynical, bitter, hateful,
and intolerant, may God rescue their students.

Part of the aim of this book to help create an intimacy and integration between the teacher and what is taught. Of course, the
quality and extent of the teacher's integrative experiences are
communicated to the students, and that is why teachers are the
focus of this book. Such intimacy is a lifelong process.

Those trained professionally and those who teach because
they have been called to teach have the same task of committing

themselves to growing and striving in ways that ensure that the message and the messenger are one. All of us struggle to integrate our Christian beliefs into our daily lives, and so I am offering encouragement to first stay on the path toward intimacy with God.

Developing a deeper relationship with God is a lifelong process. In this relationship we deepen our intimacy and strive to integrate Christian principles into our everyday lives. We know from our experiences with relationships that they require constant attention and commitment. The Christian life is no different. In the same way that our human relationships demand certain responsibilities, like sharing in the household duties, being present to each other, and participating in the life of the family, the path toward intimacy with God calls us to be a people of prayer, study, and self-reflection. In addition is the commitment to the life of the church community, the Christian family.

Teachers who believe that they are perfect make the worst teachers, and the same can be said of super-intelligent persons. However, certain flaws in a teacher would disqualify some to be teachers. Parents, rectors, and the church community must take utmost care to ensure that teachers do not cause spiritual, emotional, sexual, or psychological damage to children, youth, or adults.

We are not about promoting imperfection, but we cannot be about holding ideals that have no way of being reached. Teachers must know how to struggle and walk with their imperfections, weaknesses, and ignorance. Please note that I am not advocating divulging one's personal struggles to students in the church community. The Christian classroom is not the place to be working out one's life issues. Adults need to find the appropriate places and support groups to do their growing and learning. When we teach from a place of accepting our own struggles with God, the message we preach is more compassionate. This is where the church community needs to take a more involved role, through its staff members, in choosing teachers that are fit to carry out this ministry.

In light of this, what does it mean to imitate God? Keep in mind that we imitate God in our teaching, and God calls us constantly to follow him. It is in following Jesus that we learn to imitate him. And so the mission of Christian teachers is to point to God and say to the students, "Behold God; it does you well to follow God."

Teachers not only point to God but also act as good shepherds in the way they care for their students. Caring for our students by teaching them about life choices mirrors what Jesus did in his ministry. More than ever our churches can be places where we proclaim the joy and the necessity of following God. There seems to be a more urgent need to profess the differences that exist in the Christian way of life. We are imitators of God, not of our president, pop stars, or CEOs.

Our Scriptures tell us that God speaks to us in love and for love's sake. In addition, we learn through the Scriptures that God journeys with us and desires to be with us in the totality of our lives. We also understand that God wants us to know that we are responsible for one another. The golden rule, the greatest commandment, is that we love our neighbor as ourselves and love one another.

Jesus, whom we seek to follow, modeled a ministry of inclusivity by always stretching the understanding of who God is and who our neighbor is. The gospels speak over and over again of Jesus reaching out to the sick, the lame, the stranger, and the foreigner. In Jesus, God showed a most profound love for the poor and for those on the margins of society and religion. Jesus modeled for us a life of obedience, humility, kindness, love, and sharing. That is what we seek to teach our students in our attempts to help them imitate Jesus.

In Jesus we learn that death is not the final word. Jesus trusted God through his death, and refused to give in to the temptation to save his own life. Jesus' death opens up for us the opportunity to talk about what it means to make sacrifices or to stand up for something in this day and age. To teach an imitating of Jesus is to focus on those realities.

As teachers we try to teach the goodness, love, and grace of God. In the creation story, God's constant phrase is "it was good." This is another area in which teachers can imitate God. When we affirm the goodness of life, we are imitating God.

It is tempting to focus on the negativity and fear in our society, but those who follow Jesus believe that these are *holy* times in which we live. We are not called to focus on fear or the bad things that happen around us. Instead we are called to celebrate life in all its goodness. We celebrate the goodness of life by living good lives, lives oriented toward the good.

Christian teachers should not make the evils of today's world the center of their teaching. As Christian teachers we believe that God has redeemed the world through Jesus and continues to bring life and hope to the world. Sin and evil will always exist, but our focus should be to point to the good and encourage love, truth, and forgiveness.

Many of our students live in despair, unable to see good in the world. Many children, youth, and adults live in families being destroyed by stress, loss, poverty, separation, and pain. Such students welcome the word that there is goodness in life, particularly if witnessed to by a trusted teacher.

Wealthy children, youth, and adults, who have all they need and all the luxuries of life, may well need the Christian teacher to point out what is good. Much of what wealthy and middle-class children, youth, and adults clamor for is in fact hollow, and only serves to mask the emptiness and confusion in their lives.

Many people today no longer know what is good. To believe in the goodness, grace, and love of God is to point those out and offer them as possibilities and alternatives to going it alone. In doing this we imitate God, who is always patient, loving, and good.

Understanding Love

Another way we imitate God as teachers is in how we teach and understand love. Love gets the prize for the most overused and misused word in our language. Yet we cannot allow the secularization and commercial aspects of love to make us rip it out of Christian dictionaries. Rather we need to boldly proclaim, by living loving lives, the value of love for Christians and all people.

Christians might reclaim love by teaching love. Love and its emphasis on forgiveness needs to be mirrored in the life of the teacher: "You must love the Lord with all your heart, mind, and soul. Love your neighbor as yourself." We need not become fanatics or fundamentalists, but on this issue we could envy the fervor of some of our fundamentalist teachers. How we teach love for

God and neighbor should be an integral part of our self-evaluation.

One of our fundamental experiences of God is through grace. *Grace* is defined variously as a share in the life of God or an experience of God's loving presence that assures us that we are all children of God. Grace is the free gift of life, salvation, and hope in God. Teachers help the Christian community by pointing to the signs of grace and articulating a redemptive understanding of grace.

Teachers can help others experience grace and talk about their experiences of grace through sharing their own experiences of it. Teaching imitates God, because in its attempt to share knowledge, it invites children, youth, and adults to share in the life of God. To teach is to teach grace, which is the life of God.

Teachers point to the joys that grace brings, and like Jesus, share the good news of grace. To teach grace is to believe that *every* act of God is an act of grace, life, love, and salvation. Creation is grace, the Incarnation of Jesus is grace, and all is grace. Through God's acts of grace, we are saved.

Teachers who strive to articulate the gifts of grace and salvation show by their attempts that they are striving to be faithful disciples of Jesus. Simply put, it is to live in the presence of God and to make God present in all our actions. To be saved is to live for salvation. To live for salvation is to teach others to do the same.

Sharing in the educational process of God is to imitate God. From the moment of creation up to the present time, what we know of God is that God loves, works, and teaches. God nurtures the world by an ongoing act of sanctification. Similarly, teachers imitate God, and by doing so they nurture children, youth, and adults to know the blessings and love of God. Living for salvation is living in the knowledge that the ills of this world cannot overpower us. To live for grace and salvation is to march for justice, love, and peace. This is necessary because teaching grace involves teaching the *disgraces* of life: structural poverty, greed, oppression, sexism, and racism. To teach only the graces of life would be tantamount to Moses hearing God's call to take off his shoes and taking off only one.

For example, one of my heroes, Dom Helder Camara, the former archbishop of Recife, Brazil, spoke out against injustice and poverty constantly. He saw it as his duty to speak truth to power, but also to teach the whole church the importance of claiming its prophetic voice. He refused to accept money for the poor unless the donors were willing to accompany him and visit the poor. He often said, "When I feed the poor, they call me a saint, but when I ask why the poor are hungry, they call me a communist." Dom Helder believed that imitating God meant acting on behalf of the poor by being poor himself and by being a friend of the poor.

A teacher friend of mine always begins her classes by asking these two questions: "Where did you meet Jesus this week?" and "How were you Jesus this week?" But before getting a response from the students, she answers the question herself. I believe that what this does is create an atmosphere in which there can be open dialogue about meeting and imitating Jesus.

When we as teachers ask what it means to imitate God in creative acts, redemptive acts, acts of liberation, and acts of generosity, we get answers that lead to more commitments to the ways of God.

To imitate God is to be aware of our humanity, embrace it, share our experiences, and walk in God. As teachers know and share their lives, they will help students to know themselves and God. To know and to share is to imitate God, who is knowledge and who shares life with us. All those who receive an integrated Christian education will seek to share their lives in the church community and the world, teaching about God the way that God has taught them.

Christian education and teaching helps students become aware of their reality, their place in the church, their role in the world, and their relationship to all that exists. God's existence and presence is a reminder always of grace and unconditional love. To teach like God is to show one another that we belong to God and that God dwells in us and in our world.

A Summary Meditation

In this section I offer a few points for reflection and further thought.

We have spent considerable time reading what it means to teach and to be taught, to educate and to be educated. In moving toward our conclusion, I invite you to a final meditation, for which I recommend ample time.

Begin by reading the bulleted points below and choosing one or two of questions as focal points for your reflection. Then sit and allow yourself to become calm and quiet. See if you can bring to mind the events of your life that have brought you to this point. You may think of your birth, your baptism, high school, friendships, college, divinity school, marriage, divorce, your children, your students, your dreams, your family and friends.

As different areas of your life come to mind, ask yourself: What have I learned from this? What am I learning? What will I learn? Then focus your attention on the question(s) you selected from the list below.

Continue to sit quietly and reflect, allowing images or responses to arise.

After a few minutes ask yourself, How does all this influence my teaching? Record your answers, and remember that there is no need to rush the time of meditation.

• Wisdom is a free gift from God, and to be human is to share in this divine wisdom. From the moment of creation, however we understand it, God has given freely of the Spirit so that human beings may know God, know each other, and know how to live in relationship with God and each other. God teaches humanity in wisdom by allowing us the freedom to accept or reject the very Wisdom of God.
   • *How do I see the wisdom of God in my own life?*
• Education has always been a part of humanity. Most ancient societies have structured themselves around the educational process. For the Greeks education served as a means of nurtur-

ing the whole society by leading all members to the good, the true, and the beautiful. For Africans education helps all the members of the village to understand the nature of things and to order right living in the community. The Jews see education as a mandate from God, and they take an active part in their education by encouraging all members to read the Torah. The Asian emphasis is on corporate growth and the contribution the individual makes to community living.

- *How does education form part of my life and my Christian community?*
- Teaching demands study, preparation, openness, and intimacy with the material being taught. To teach is to know oneself, to know the students, and to know the subject, in our case, God. Teaching must involve an integration of all three aspects and a willingness to share in the lives of the students and to share God by sharing one's life with the students.
  - *As a teacher, how would I evaluate my study, my openness, my life experience, and my knowledge of my subject?*
- Teaching and education imply a process of leading students to truth, by leading the truth out of them. To lead the truth out of a student is to first honor the truth that exists in the student. A teacher has to be willing to live this truth and to lead the truth out of his or her heart.
  - *Where do I hope to lead my students?*
- To teach is to create an experience of grace. Christian teachers need to reaffirm the power of grace in the Christian community. At the same time, there can be no teaching about grace without referring to the disgraces of life.
  - *What are the disgraces in society that I leave out of my teaching?*
- Greeks use the question, Africans the story, Jews the Torah, and Asians poems and riddles as teaching tools. To teach , we need tools or methods. For each method we discussed, we showed how the questions informed the story and created new stories.
  - *What method do I use as a teacher?*
- Much of our discussion has focused on the importance of the teacher having self-knowledge. If we do not know ourselves, we will teach from our blind spots, and if we do not reflect on the

things we do, we will continue to make mistakes. Jamaicans say, "Check yourself, before you wreck yourself."
- *How do I evaluate my activities as a teacher and as a person?*
- We discussed education as being dynamic, reciprocal, and exciting.
  - *How do I remain excited about my teaching ministry?*
  - *Where do I find encouragement from my students?*
  - *What do I need to keep doing or where do I need to grow in my teaching ministry?*
- Teachers point to the self, the church community, and the world. A good Christian education is one that allows students to live their lives responsibly in their relationships with self, the church, and the world. Teaching helps unmask the fallacies that popular culture and nationalism perpetuate.
  - *How am I influenced by the consumerism, denial, greed, pleasure, work, or power that is so much a part of society?*
  - *What might I do to move beyond them?*
- God is our teacher. The activity of God in this world, especially expressed through Jesus, teaches us that God is love and is concerned with the world. God's creative act was the most important lesson in our lives as Christians. In the Incarnation of Jesus, we learn what it is to enter fully into the realities of our world.
  - *How do I allow God to teach me about loving my neighbor and the world?*
  - *How do I teach about God?*

II

Teaching for Life
Womb-to-Tomb Formation

6 The Child as Student and Teacher

Introductory Meditations

We begin this chapter on teaching as a life ministry by meditating on our lives. Find a quiet spot where you can sit undisturbed for a few moments.

Imagine that you are near the end of your life, and you have just twenty minutes before you die. Look over the people, things, and events that fill you with gratitude. Be as still as you can be, and notice what comes to mind. Spend at least ten minutes with this meditation before going on to the questions. Offer up a prayer of thanksgiving for all the things that have happened in your life.

Continue to look over your life, prayerfully going over all the events. Which moments stand out? Why? Look at the things, places, and people that have caused you hurt, pain, sadness, and anger. Can you let go? How? Can you forgive? How? What decisions in your life would you make differently? In what way? Think of all that you have learned. Is there something else that you wish you had learned? something you wish you had taught someone? If you could determine your final thought or prayer, what would it be?

This meditation is like an examen, the difference being that it reviews one's entire life and not just a day or a moment. It encourages us to view our lives as teachers within the overall formation of our lives. See if you can make some time today, tomorrow, or next week to be alone and do this meditation. You can come back to this meditation and use it anytime in your life, or for the rest of your life.

These questions will serve as a means of examining your role as teacher and how teachers have influenced you:

What lessons have prepared me for life and death, and how?
Which of my parents taught me the most about life, and how?
Which of my children or friends has taught me the most about life, and how?
What lesson did I learn as a child that still guides my life?
What lesson did I learn as an adolescent that still guides my life?
Which lessons did I learn as an adult that guide my life?
What has the death of a relative or friend taught me about life and death?

Please take ample time with these questions, because there is no way of answering them properly without time. These questions will help us look at our reaction to death and how we have been affected by death. What death does to us determines our posture in life. An honest reflection on death, therefore, will influence how we teach life.

Now I invite you to spend some time on the following passages. Allow the words to find a home in you by rereading them, coming back to them, and, most of all, praying them.

Truly you have formed my inmost being;
you knit me deep in my mother's womb.
I give you thanks that I am so fearfully,
wonderfully made;
wonderful are your works.
My soul also you knew full well;
nor was my frame unknown to you
when I was made in the deepest secret,
when I was fashioned in the depths of the earth.
     (Adapted from Psalm 139:13–15)

In my beginning
I find my end
Lest I believe in darkness
I find my light
Death may hold my hands
I find life guides my feet.

Jesus said to all:
"Whoever wishes to be my follower
that is to follow me every day
must deny self, take up the cross each day,
and follow in my steps
every day.
To try and save your life is to lose it.
To lose your life is to save it.
What profit is there
in gaining the whole world
and losing your soul?
If you are ashamed of me and my teachings
I will be ashamed of you
when I come in glory."
        (Adapted from Luke 9:23–26)

All day we die
Yet we fear death
Yes
Death
Does sting
It can't help itself
Only life can help us
and itself, all day.

The Child as Student and Teacher

Children participate in the Christian community as eager learners, but adults miss the significance of their presence if children are not seen as members who share in the teaching ministry. Children have a special place in the Christian community because they witness to the reality of what it means to be human and to grow.

We all were children at some point. As simple as this may sound, my experience is that many of the problems we adult church members have with children stem from our unique ability to forget that we too once were children. When church communities refuse to learn from their children, they make a grave mistake. Church communities spend too much time trying to teach children rather than learning from them.

Education involves a serious engagement of subjects by partners who feel respected and honored for their gifts. When church communities honor and respect children, children will begin to teach important lessons about the spiritual life. For this reason the church must keep searching for ways to listen to the experiences of its members. After all, together we are one body in Christ; we cannot do without one another. A question parishes must face is whether much of the education process becomes a way of silencing children, youth, and adults, or whether it is a way of creating dialogue. This is especially true for children, because adults have the inclination to believe that "children should be seen and not heard."

Like the Greek questions, the African stories, the Jewish Torah, and Asian poems and riddles, Christian education methods must engage children in a relationship that allows for mutual teaching and learning. Much of what is being done in the area of the religious education of the child focuses on exercises to aid the child's imagination. Children are encouraged to think, ponder, and wonder about God. When we listen to their reflections, we learn much about God.

In these moments of listening to the child, a good teacher will help guide the child's reflection. As a teacher it may be important to encourage, praise, and accept what the child says; but it is just as important to communicate the right message about God's love for the child and other children.

Those who teach children somehow need to communicate a love for Jesus and God's love for the children they teach. As teachers listen, over time they will get a sense of the appropriate guidance needed by each child. It is in listening to the child that we realize that each child responds differently to God and the church. As children, they need to learn and live the reality of being accepted unconditionally by God, who created them differently.

The end goal of every conversation in the church is that it leads to a better relationship with Jesus. Jesus as a child, Jesus as a friend, Jesus as a healer, Jesus as a caring person, and Jesus as a storyteller are themes about Jesus that will delight children and encourage them to find in Jesus a friend who loves them.

Church communities and teachers reveal to the child what it means to be loved by God in a special way. Children reveal to the teachers and church community that God moves in mysterious, delightful, and unpredictable ways. It is for this reason that the child belongs in the church both as potential student and teacher. The teacher's approach to the child is to become like the child in a posture of being potential teacher and student. I think the greatest metaphor for this is the relationship that a parent has with a child.

When a child is born, mother and child continue the journey of teaching and learning from each other. This journey alters and interrupts the life of the mother. Most families who experience the joy of a newborn will also confess to the ways the child changes everything. Sleeping and eating patterns in the child are two of the things that often teach new ways of being to those who are attending to the child. Church communities learn much about themselves and their ministries by examining the ways children change its worship, ministry, and mission.

Before beginning this section on the role of the child in the Christian community as learner and teacher, let us spend some time with a passage from Scripture.

Read the story of Samuel (1 Samuel 3:1–11). Close your eyes and imagine that you are Samuel. Experience yourself being called by God and going to a parent, friend, or teacher. Pay attention to what you feel or sense as you sleep in the temple and hear your name being called.

You might repeat this meditation by imagining that you are Eli or God.

As usual, here are a few questions to aid you in praying this passage: Who speaks in this passage? Who listens in this passage? What does Samuel teach Eli? What does Eli teach Samuel? What does God teach both Samuel and Eli? With whom do I identify more? What is God calling me to do or teach? How do I help or teach my students to listen to God?

The story of Samuel poignantly reminds the Christian community that the place for the child is within the church. Exegetes may disagree with my literal interpretation of this passage, but I want to hold to an interpretation that suggests that the adult and the child belong in church together. It is obvious from the passage that Samuel is comfortable in the temple. He sleeps in the temple, and seems to be at total ease with himself and the surroundings.

Does your church offer that comfort level to children? I am not talking about just physical space, but also about relationships that we foster with children in our churches. Do children feel comfortable in the church? Do children feel comfortable around the people in the church? Do adults want children in the church? Do adults feel comfortable with children in the church?

One Christmas I invited a church community to bring a newborn and place him at the foot of the altar. As we read the Christmas story from the gospel, the child started crying. I reached over and picked up the child and continued reading the gospel. The child kept crying, but many of the parishioners were in tears. They made the leap to realizing that the Child Jesus must have cried. Many later said it was their best experience of Christmas in church.

But let us return to our discussion of Samuel. Samuel needed Eli to help him discern God's will. Let us note that it was not Eli who called Samuel, but God. When teachers or the community relate to children, our work is to point them to God, a God who is already calling them from within.

Oftentimes adults in the church take their jobs so seriously that they forget it is *God* who needs to call the child. I have met church-school teachers who are at the point of a breakdown because the children are not coming to church school or to church. After five minutes with these well-meaning folks, I find that I can sympathize with the children for not wanting to come to church school or church.

One cannot examine the relationships between the adult and the child or the church community and the child without examining how present-day Christians view behavior in church. Many adults believe that in church a child should never talk, never ask questions, but should be as still as still can be.

This is a good time to pause and pray the Prayers for the Candidates for Baptism, found in the Book of Common Prayer. Repeat this prayer slowly two or three times, and make an effort to repeat one line to yourself throughout the day.

Deliver them, O Lord, from the way of sin and death.
Open their hearts to your grace and truth.
Fill them with your holy and life-giving Spirit.
Keep them in the faith and communion of your holy Church.
Teach them to love others in the power of the Spirit.
Send them into the world in witness to your love.
Bring them to the fullness of your peace and glory.

Grant, O Lord, that all who are baptized into the death of Jesus Christ your Son may live in the power of his resurrection and look for him to come again in glory; who lives and reigns now and forever. Amen. (pp. 305–306, responses omitted)

Be sure to spend some quiet time later in the day mulling over these words. Reflect on what each line means, and then consider the following questions:
• Who has taught me to understand these words?
• Who teaches me to understand these words?
• How do I teach these words? How do these words affect my life as a Christian?
• How do they affect my life as a Christian teacher?

Remember to take notes, discuss your responses with someone, or draw something in response. It is very important that we get in touch with how we teach and from where we teach.

Adults fool themselves into believing that silence means a person is paying attention. Having preached to and worked with many adults, I know that silence does not mean agreement, attention, or mental alertness. I prefer the child's fidgeting to the false blank stares of adults who are pretending to be holy, pretending to agree, and pretending to having raised better children than those now misbehaving in church.

Let us, as church, move to a point where we welcome the voice, giggles, and chatter of children as joyful noise. Children, in order to feel at home in the church, need to know they have a place and a voice in church. How many adults immediately tell the child to be quiet, even before the lips of the child begin to open?

This attitude may arise from a misconception about comportment in church, a Victorian holdover about their being seen and not heard. If we pay attention to the story of Samuel and Eli, we see that Eli is able to point Samuel to God because Samuel has the chance to speak.

When we educate children for life, we give them a voice in church, without interfering. When we ask them questions about life and God, we help them to wonder about God and life, and we allow them to speak. For instance, when we gather with children instead of praying for them, we might find ways for them to express their own prayers.

Prayer comes naturally to children and they pray about mundane, ridiculous, and troubling things, but in wonderful ways. A young child, after being invited to lead the Lord's Prayer, began like this, "Our Father, how do you know my name?" In this child's interpretation of the Lord's Prayer was a passageway to discussing the power of God's knowledge of each of us.

Often we want children to speak, but we want them to speak in the way we want. Adults have created a fantasy about how children should speak. That problem is more obvious in multicultural settings. Adults would rather children *speak properly,* or not speak at all. Children speak in their own ways and in their own time. Church communities must be places that allow children the opportunity to speak when they want, and, yes, how they want.

As children find their voices in the church community, they do so along with the youth and the adults. In the story of Eli and Samuel, we see the respect and love that they hold for each other. Children can learn how to respect the wisdom of youth and adults in the parish, but by the same token, youth and adults must respect the children.

All members of the family can teach and learn new things about life, the world, the church, and God. I would argue that the church community fails in its mission if it cannot facilitate a learning process that calls for a mutual exchange and for listening to each other's experience (or lack of experience) of God.

Why do we suppose that God used the child Samuel as a messenger? God called Samuel because God knew he would respond. Children respond to God because they know God. Children have fewer apprehensions about saying the correct thing. A child in one parish I visited said, "Loving God, burst my heart with love for you." Imagine that! What would it be like for an adult to say that prayer every day? Another way to encourage children's prayer is to have them design prayer cards. They will delight us with their vivid imagination and creativity.

I do not want to romanticize the lives of children, because I have been outside North American countries and seen how Third World children live and die. Many children are sold into prostitution by age eight. In Brazil over a million children live on the street, not to mention the plight of children in Africa and India.

Even in the most miserable of circumstances, a child is still a child and still possesses childlike qualities that can bring adults to tears or gales of laughter. A child has a quality that speaks of being known by God, loved by God, and blessed by God. Of course, we are all known by God, but it seems to me that children are known and loved by God in a special way. The Gospels point to a tenderness that God displays uniquely toward the child. The disciples chased the children away, but Jesus rebukes the disciples and calls the children to him.

Think of the many children who are sent away by world leaders and those in power, and we will better understand the activity of God in those moments. God seeks a way to embrace children who are abandoned by the structures of power in society. How can we be there for them?

When churches send children outside or to the basement, or refuse them full membership in the church, we need to be reminded that Jesus is always calling the children back, to be with him. When societies ignore the rights of children, when governments abandon children and invest in weapons, we as a Christian community can know where God stands and how God reacts. When the Christian community turns children away, God calls them to the center and uses them to teach the adults. God knows the true place and the plight of the child in today's church and society.

We are all loved. And yet we know that God loves the child in a special way. A close examination of Jesus' life shows him reaching out to those who are most vulnerable and those who are on the margins. God has a preferential love for children, because in our society and in the church, they are the most at risk.

If God has a preferential option for the children of the world because they are more at risk, I believe that children who are poor and dying of hunger are even more precious to God. Earlier I mentioned the need for comprehensive education. The church needs to teach that poor and dying children are precious to God; it is even more important to teach this fact to children.

Children in wealthy parishes must be taught about the poor children of the world and God's love for them. To teach with integrity is to teach that we are all members of God's family.

We are all blessed. To be created, redeemed, and sanctified by God is to be blessed. Taking all this into consideration, even the fact that God loves all people equally, I believe that God has a special love for children.

When educators and teachers recognize this fact, they will treat children differently. And if church communities live from this standpoint, then all the angst over children disturbing worship will begin to dissipate. Children identify with adults, see their worth in the eyes of adults, and look to adults for meaning. If adults can reflect what it means to be blessed by God during worship, then children will have a better sense of themselves as blessed.

It is important to realize that this is truly a family affair: families modeling God's love for the child in the home, and the church family modeling God's love for the child in the church and in society. It is in church where children see their parents offering a handshake, the greeting of peace, hugs and kisses—sometimes to complete strangers.

There is no better message to give children than that they are known, loved, and blessed by God. Teachers are called to share this good news with children, and to help them learn how to respond to it. I suspect that children feel loved, known, and blessed quite naturally.

How unfortunate that adults often unwittingly communicate their doubts, fears, or even their refusal or inability to accept themselves as loved, known, and blessed. It is more unfortunate when this is communicated in the church community, a place where intimacy, love, and blessings should abound. Teachers in the church community must not only point children to what God has already done and is doing in the lives of children; adults must be willing to pay attention and learn from the presence of God in the lives of children.

A Watering Hole

Is there a difference between the baptismal commitment of an adult and that of a child? What significance does my Baptism have in my daily life? What are my views about children's full participation in church? What do children teach me?

List ten things you would or would not teach children in the church. Spend some time with the items on your list, and ask yourself why you listed each one.

Those who teach or parent children may want to memorize this prayer from the Book of Common Prayer, *829.*

Prayer for the care of children

Almighty God, heavenly Father, you have blessed us with the joy
and care of children: Give us calm strength and patient wisdom as
we bring them up, that we may teach them to love whatever is just
and true and good, following the example of our Savior Jesus Christ.
Amen.

7 The Youth in the Church Community as Student and Teacher

Introductory Meditations

Naaman, the army commander of the king of Aram, was highly respected and loved by his master, for through him the Lord had given victory to Aram. But brave as Naaman was, the man was a leper. Now the Arameans had captured from the land of Israel a little girl, who became the maidservant of Naaman's wife. "If only my master would present himself to the prophet in Samaria," she said to her mistress, "he would cure him of his leprosy." Naaman went and told his lord just what the slave girl from the land of Israel had said. (Adapted from 2 Kings 5:1–4)

The Lord said to Samuel: "How long will you mourn and weep for Saul, whom I have rejected as king of Israel? Fill your horn with oil now, and be on your way. I am sending you to Jesse of Bethlehem, for I have chosen my king from his sons." . . . Then Samuel asked Jesse, "Are these all the sons you have?" Jesse replied, "There is still the youngest, who is tending the sheep." Samuel said to Jesse, "Send for him; we will not begin the sacrificial banquet until he arrives here." Jesse had the young man brought to them. He was ruddy, a youth handsome to behold and making a splendid appearance. The Lord said, "There—anoint him, for this is he!" (Adapted from 1 Samuel 16:1,11–12)

Before going any further, let us pause to do some reflection and meditation on these two passages. If possible, set aside two different times for this, one to focus on the young girl and another on the young man in the passages.

Cure of Naaman: Sit in a quiet spot and read the passage slowly. Put the book down and allow the passage to unfold in your mind. Find your favorite word, phrase, or sentence in the passage, and ask the Lord what relevance it has in your life.

Spend some moments asking yourself: Where is the leprosy in my church, family, work, or country? Where is the army commander in my church, family, work, or country? Where is the young girl? How does the young girl know the information she shares?

Ask the Spirit of God to give you a heart that is open to youth. Return to the passage and read it once again. Focus your attention on the young girl, and ask: What does she look like? What is she feeling? How does she speak? What do you suppose she is thinking as she speaks? What happens to her after this?

Call of David: Take a few minutes to reread the passage in its entirety—1 Samuel 16:1–13. Spend time noticing the words of Samuel. Allow these words to find a place in your heart.

Read the passage on David slowly, and allow the events to run through your mind. Put yourself in the story first as Jesse, then as Samuel, and finally as David.

As Jesse, try to get in touch with your initial enthusiasm, disappointment, reluctance, and acceptance. As Samuel, see if you can experience letting go of your desires or wishes, your plans. What does it mean to do what God wants? Imagine that you are David, out on the margin doing your own thing, and suddenly being called by God. What does it feel like?

Spend some time reflecting on the youth throughout the world. Why are some chosen while some remain on the outside? Think of your students, and ask yourself what draws you to one student and not another. Who are the youth left outside? What is needed to listen to them? How can we, and how can you, invite estranged youth into the life of the church?

The Youth in the Church Community as Student and Teacher

One of the greatest anguishes faced by many parishes is: Why don't young people come to church? What can we do to attract young people to the church? Why aren't young people participating? These questions remind me of a story, which I am delighted to share with you:

> A woman on her way home came upon a friend, who was obviously searching for something. She stopped and said to her friend, "Tom, what are you looking for?" "I have lost my key," Tom replied. "I will help you look," Kathy said. After about an hour, Kathy said to Tom, "Where did you lose your key?" "Over there," Tom replied. Kathy was furious, "For God's sake, why on earth are we looking here?" "Because we have more light here."

The greatest mission of those vested with the duties of educating or forming in the church is to find in the members the life of the wider community. Youth, often neglected because of an overemphasis on children's and adult ministries, need to know that the teachers and youth leaders in the church see in them the key to what it means to be church.

When church communities forget their most important mission of educating the youth, they engage in spiritual abandonment that can have far-reaching consequences for the young person and the community. Education and formation, teaching and nurturing are elements of church life that require an ongoing commitment from cradle to grave.

I offer this as a proposal: that if education and nurturing were viewed as a ministry for the whole family of God, parishes would not be left wondering where the youth have gone. And parishes who invest time being present to young people, listening to them and nurturing them, may well ask these questions, but they will have a very different tone to their questions.

How children and youth are nurtured, welcomed, listened to, and given space in the church determine how the youth feel drawn to the church. If a church community does not welcome children and youth and sees children and youth as a bother, the youth will not come back. We really should get over ourselves, you know, because we know the old adage, "Children live what they learn."

To keep youth in the church, we have to inform, educate, and nurture them. But just as important is the church's need to be informed, educated, and nurtured by the youth. One way of engaging the youth in worship is to have them plan the service at least once a month. They get to choose the music and the readings. I believe that it is important that the planning be done using the traditional form of worship as a framework, but that the youth be given leeway to be as creative as they desire. When we encourage the youth to participate, we encourage them to participate as members of our particular congregations, and so it is important that they know the tradition to which they belong. As they plan the liturgy, they will, for sure, grapple with understanding the way things are done. Our liturgies have a form to them that is based in an age-old tradition, but the rubrics allow us to be creative with how we express various aspects of the liturgy.

To ensure that our youth return to church, we have to engage them, learn their interpretations of the gospels, learn their needs for God, and learn their form of worship.

I suspect that few youth find church an appealing, welcoming place to be. And I believe that this is where we should start as a church community when we ask ourselves about educating the youth. Teachers teach best when they make it their bounden duty to learn from youth what motivates them, what challenges them, what gives them hope, what fascinates them, and what causes them pain. A simple way of doing this is to engage in the process of faith sharing or life sharing. Whenever youth gather in the church, these three questions might help them grow in their faith: How are you today? Where do you experience God's love? What might God be calling you to do, be, or say?

There is no nurturing of the youth by teachers or the church community without treating the youth as subjects. By this I mean respecting the lives of the youth and being able to take off our shoes before them—to reveal ourselves and to allow them to reveal who they really are.

In the same way that children need to be welcomed into the

church, youth need to know that they are wanted in and by the church community. To let young people know that they are appreciated means dealing with issues, from the pulpit and in encounters with them, that concern their lives. Sexuality, drugs, peer pressure, violence, racism, meaning, friendship, love, fear, and human development are relevant issues that need to be discussed by the Christian teacher of youth. When the youth have a voice to talk about their issues, they might pay attention to what adults, teachers, and the wider church community have to say. Having youth forums in church, where young people get a chance to share on these topics, is a wonderful way to make the church a welcoming and respectful place.

Like David many young people live on the margins of society and the church. Unlike David, often no one makes the commitment to go after them, to seek them out, or, like Samuel, to anoint them. Many teachers within the church spend time inside the church wondering why young people do not come to church or find church meaningful.

My friend Caroline Fairless says that the best way to begin is to start from the assumption that children and youth belong in church. To hold that they belong is to admit that they have as much of a claim on every aspect of the church as do the altar guild and the adult members.

The more church communities can welcome and listen to the voices of the children and youth, the more they approximate communities where justice is lived out. Church communities flourish when they become places where we take risks to discover how God may be calling us to something new. A political saying in Brazil went like this: "Try something! Invent something! Do something different this year." That could be a great mantra for our church communities in regard to the youth.

Much of our discussion on education focuses on the dynamic and dialectical nature of education. In order to learn the needs of youth and what makes them excited, church-school teachers or church leaders must allow youth to teach them. It is quite simple: church communities must believe that youth are also the body of Christ. Like Jesus teaching in the temple, youth can bring a greater understanding of the challenges facing the Christian community.

Yet there is no way to learn from the youth except to locate them, stand before them, and be willing to listen to them. Before we begin to teach, we must begin to listen. We need to listen to the youth where they are and where they want to be. I cannot imagine how a church can call itself a community of believers if it knows nothing about the home, school, and life of its youth.

Here are some suggestions that churches might find helpful as they think about working with youth:

- Visit youth in the gathering places to which they are naturally attracted, such as sporting events. Church staff must take care not to cause any discomfort in the youth by their presence.
- Organize a movie trip.
- Watch videos at the home of a church member.
- Organize sleepovers.
- Plan fun games.
- Have seasonal parties.
- Organize home visits.

We learn from youth when we visit them at home. How a youth lives his or her adolescence in the home will help determine his or her presence in the church. Teachers and youth workers must find ways to make home visits a regular part of youth work and formation. Priests, youth leaders, and teachers do not work against the home, but in conjunction with the family of the youth.

Parents must also feel encouraged to visit the youth groups or church-school classes for the youth. While it is important that the youth be informed about adult visits, it should never be a rule that parents or other adults are not welcome. This is one way to encourage the health of the family, because the church community is never one to interfere with family—except to intervene if the family has destructive patterns and habits.

It is also just as important to listen to youth talk about their experience at school. I would suggest that no form of education for children, youth, or adults should ever begin without asking about the events, happy or sad, in the lives of those who are gathered. What happens at school has tremendous importance if we are to learn from our youth and educate them to take their places in society as Christians.

Family and school are important loci in the lives of our youth. Their neighborhoods, malls, clubs, friends, and computers are places that the church, church-school teachers, and youth leaders would do well to be familiar with. Youth bring all they are and fear to us as teachers, and we must listen to them. By our companionship, by our listening and care, we are demonstrating for them a Jesus and a God who are interested in who they are.

To bring their lives to prayer, to bring their concerns into the Christian classroom is to honor them and share in the things they find important. The story about David reminds us that many in the family, school, or church are seen as members, but for whatever reason, may not be inside when the prophet comes knocking. Jesse, David's father, presented seven sons, and never thought of his youngest son, David.

Some time ago I met a priest who was having problems in his parish. He kindly informed me that things had been so busy in the parish that he and the vestry had had no time for the youth and the children in the parish. "There are many other things we need to get in place," he told me. I told him that the youth were the most important ministry in his parish. The more we spoke, the more he realized that the problems the parish was facing were all connected to how the youth were being treated. The priest and vestry, in truth the whole parish, did not see the need to go outside and call in the youth. Little did they know that they were preventing the growth of their parish, preventing new life.

After visiting them over a period of twelve months, I was able to convince them of the importance of looking into providing child care, fixing up a youth room, and having a more inclusive liturgy. I still receive postcards from the parish thanking me for helping them to be a more welcoming parish. They had made the leap of faith, and suddenly families were coming out of the woodwork.

A Watering Hole

Maybe this is a good time to stop and meditate on our experiences when we were adolescents in the church.

Spend at least fifteen minutes on this meditation, writing down your thoughts after you finish the meditation.

Begin by asking the Holy Spirit to enlighten you and journey with you. A useful mantra is "Come and fill me, O Holy Spirit." You might want to repeat this several times. I invite you to revisit your life, picturing yourself at thirteen years of age. Spend sufficient time examining your life from thirteen to nineteen. You may want to focus on the most difficult periods during those years. Remember to revisit this period with the Spirit's guidance, because you may discover painful things in your life.

As a youth, how did you feel about yourself or about life? What were your views on sex, music, God, church, your rector, your parents, and your friends?

Try to remember what impact church had on your life, and why. Spend some time trying to recall your best friend or another youth you knew. What role did God, church school, religious education, and the church play in her or his life? Did you like going to church as a youth? Where was God in your life?

A poem, a prayer, a drawing, or a conversation with a friend may be a good way to finish this meditation. Remember, we cannot teach the youth unless we know them and know ourselves as youth.

I encourage you to repeat this meditation over the next few days, each time inviting the Spirit to walk with you as you visit your life as a youth.

8 A Tool for Discussion: What Do You Think?

The content of this chapter will provide discussion for those who work in Christian education in the parish. The ideas for discussion can serve as part of an ongoing discussion in parishes on a weekly or monthly basis.

A. Welcome participants and use an icebreaker as a way of doing introductions. I suggest using an icebreaker that is somehow connected to the theme of the day and that is not distracting.

B. Outline for the group the plan for the day. Handouts might be useful, as they can help people not be too anxious about what is coming next.

C. Divide into groups of three or four, and hand each group the same paragraph for discussion.

D. Ask the groups to answer two questions about their discussion idea: What is this passage saying to me? What is this passage calling me to be?

E. Invite the groups to come back together, and allow further time for sharing as a group.

F. Invite people to go off alone for fifteen to thirty minutes and reflect on a Scripture passage. Here are a few suggestions: Genesis 1:1–20, Exodus 3:1–12, Exodus 13:14–16, Deuteronomy 6:4–9, Psalm 23, Psalm 62, Psalm 100, Psalm 139, Matthew 28:18–20, Luke 10:25–37, John 14:1–10.

G. Invite the participants to come back and share their reflection experiences in the same small group they were in before.

H. Close with prayer.

Discussion Ideas

1. We cannot educate youth or give them their rightful place in the church if we do not understand them. Understanding youth, which means knowing where they are, is a difficult task, but it is a lot easier if the adults can access their own experiences as youth. Adults who remember their own experience should not pretend to be experts on youth culture, but instead should open themselves up to listening to the experience of the youth. When an adult (educator) prays and reflects on his or her experience as a youth, the task of listening to the youth is made easier.

2. When we listen to our youth and when we leave what we are doing to seek them out, we open up our ministries to untold wonders.

3. Great things can happen when we give our children and youth their rightful places in the church. For youth to have their rightful place in the church is for them to have a voice, a chance to speak, and many occasions to be heard. Youth must be reminded that their place in the church community is also one where they can teach the church what is happening in the world. The church community, of all places, cannot be one where youth are ignored or left on the margins.

4. If the church community listens to the youth, the youth will listen to them. Once again it is important to recall the model of education practiced by the Greeks, Jews, Africans, and Asians: based on a commitment to engagement, these people treated their philosophy, their literature, and their stories as subjects.

5. When we give youth the space to be subjects, we allow them to engage us by sharing about their lives, their families, their schools, their friendships, their fears, their sins, their joys, and their love. In short, we make them welcome.

6. Teachers in the church community must find ways to secure the voices of young people. Youth in the church have for too long been relegated to the margins; they are kept outside the main events and decisions of the church community. Too often church leaders only pay attention when it is too late; youth become the center of discussion when their numbers have dropped. As long as youth come to church in abundance, most adults do not care if they participate or not.

7. The teaching ministry of the church will forever undermine itself if youth are expected to grow into full members of Christ's body without being encouraged to take responsibility in the church or without input into the vestry's actions or the habitual ways of doing things.

8. Youth should read, preach, serve as Eucharistic ministers, and serve on church committees—not only on special occasions, but all the time. If we believe that we are all equal members of the family of God or the body of Christ, then we must see Christ as the child, the youth, and the adult. It is no longer Christian to have all the ministries in the church carried out by adults.

9. When we open up avenues for the youth to participate, we learn about what it means to be a youth in today's world. Youth are struggling to fit in, find their identity, break loose from their parents, wrestle with studies, challenge authority, experiment with life— even life without church. A teacher in the church must address those issues, first by encouraging the youth to own and express the experiences.

10. The task of listening to youth is not always easy, because many of us do not have the experience of having been listened to as youth. Those in charge of youth formation must provide meaningful activities for youth, where they can say, feel, and be the things that matter to them.

11. Teachers can explore with youth what it means to grow as a human being in a social, spiritual, and psychological sense. Youth in the church need to experience themselves as having an important function, role, and presence in the church.

12. The church and teachers must help youth express their opinions, skepticism, dreams, and nightmares. Teachers must be seen as people who "talk the talk and walk the walk." Those who teach must live the Christian life; they need not be perfect, but they do need to be people of morality, justice, hope, and faith.

13. Teachers can represent for the youth what it means to strive for righteousness, love, justice, and inclusion. Imagine the wonderful possibilities if youth could engage the holy heart of the teacher and the teacher could engage the growing heart of the youth.

14. Teachers must listen, show understanding, express compassion, speak the truth boldly, and offer the gospel as containing options for life.

15. Youth can be encouraged to see the role of the church community as providing guidance, forgiveness, hope, and love. We hope that the church community will give the youth a sense of what it means to belong to a spiritual community, a family that is larger than their own but not in competition with it.

16. Teachers in the church must not get stuck in the church. By this I mean that they must envision that part of their work continues in the homes. Church-school teachers or youth leaders need to visit the homes of their youth. Proper boundaries need to be maintained, but it is necessary that the teachers get to know the parents of the youth. If the parents do not come to church, teachers must extend a personal welcome to them and also describe the church-school's or youth group's mission statement.

17. In teaching youth, there is no better message to spread than this: They are valued and they have companionship for their faith story. Teachers are called to help articulate within and with the youth the spiritual, theological, physical, psychological, and social dimensions of life.

18. Church teachers can encourage youth to learn what it is to live and believe in Jesus. Earlier I mentioned that education allows the individual to move beyond himself or herself. Christian education needs to open the youth to the lives and experiences of young people of other races, means, lifestyles, orientations, and countries.

19. Church communities must be places where the youth feel affirmed, encouraged, and loved. Church communities can foster in youth what it means to hope for a better tomorrow, what it means to dream. Too many youth feel no hope for the future.

20. Teachers teach best by assuring the youth that they will stand with them and search with them. Teachers also teach best by encouraging youth to see themselves as evangelizers and leaders. When youth lead and evangelize, the church community is in a good position to call itself the whole people of God.

21. Some people believe that the life and meaning of the church can only take place within the confines of the church on Sundays. In the same way that the prophet Samuel went outside to find David, teachers of religious education will need to find ways of connecting with the youth at school and at home. Sometimes the only connection might be allowing the youth to talk about life at school and at home.

22. It is important to remember that the stories of the youth are mirrored in the biblical stories. In the stories of the youth, the teacher will discover the presence of God in the life of the students and so can mirror this back to them.

23. When possible, youth should be encouraged to talk about their faith at school. As the youth mature in the church community we hope they will become more cognizant of their baptismal vows. Youth belong to God, according to our understanding of God and our baptismal vows. We tend to forget to remind our youth of their baptismal promises.

24. It falls on the teacher and the church community to find healthy ways to infuse daily Christian life with reminders of the baptismal covenant shared by all Christians. Owning their baptismal commitments need not be a guilt-ridden experience for youth. Christian education is at its best when youth feel as proud of their faith and church as they are of their family.

25. In Christian education we attempt to draw out of youth the life of Christ that resides in them. We do this best by mirroring in the home and church what it means to be children of God. Do you renounce all sinful desires that draw you from the love of God? Do you turn to Jesus and accept him as your Savior? Do you put your whole trust in his grace and love?

26. When we encourage our youth to own their Christian faith, we can affect their attitudes at school and at home. We also hope to allow the youth to educate us by listening to their experience in the school and the home. It is important that adults allow the input of youth, especially about what happens at school, to affect how they teach and what they teach.

27. It would be a tragedy if the church were to continue to lose relevance for youth. In August 2000, two million youth from across the world gathered in Rome for a pilgrimage. Many Vatican officials took pride in the gathering, declaring that it was a spiritual Woodstock. The Vatican boasted that it had gathered one of the largest groups of youth in recent times for a spiritual cause.

28. Few denominations have a religious figure like the pope or an infrastructure capable of gathering two million youth, but what we can learn from this is that youth will respond—if we invite them. If our churches take time to give youth the voice and the space they need to be church, we will certainly succeed in drawing them into Christ and in drawing Christ out of them.

29. What it means to educate the youth in church is to somehow excite them enough about their own faith that they will proclaim it, find meaning in it, and educate others about it. To get to this point, the church, parents, and religious educators must help youth see the importance of their baptismal vows, the relevance of the Bible, and the integrity of Christian ethics.

30. Youth must be encouraged to live as Jesus did by choosing life, being generous, serving others, respecting their peers, resisting evil, doing acts of charity, living merciful lives, and seeking to draw others to a life of love. Youth must learn this from the church, even as they teach the church and educators new ways of being Christian.

31. In teaching youth, the heart of the message is the discovery that they are loved unconditionally by God. Teachers can help youth explore this unconditional love by encouraging them to look at their relationships with their parents, friends, and church. Teachers in the church community must work closely with parents to communicate spiritual values, especially a love for the Bible. Educators of youth must point to God's love and encourage the youth to choose a path that includes love, a search for justice, and gospel values. For this the Bible is a handy and faithful companion.

A Watering Hole

Make a list of the spiritual, psychological, and emotional challenges that you believe youth face today. What answers, responses, or challenges does a religious education or faith in Jesus bring to these issues?

Think about the church's liturgy, and compare it with popular music on the radio. As you spend time thinking about this, you might want to consider how the church viewed youth differently ten, twenty, or thirty years ago. Invite the Spirit to journey with you back into your adolescent years.

How were you influenced by popular culture? What were your views about God, the church, and religious education? Some of us may discover that we didn't even think about these things; I suspect that some of today's youth may not think about them either. Some of us may discover that we thought about these things all the time; I suspect many young people today do too.

Now spend some time answering the following questions: What lessons do I teach about a personal commitment to God? How do I as an educator listen to the youth? How does my church community listen to the youth? How do I support the youth in the family and the church? What are my dreams for young people in the church? How do I welcome youth in the church?

Those who teach young persons might want to spend some time praying this prayer, even memorizing it.

God our Father, you see your children growing up in an unsteady and confusing world: Show them that your ways give more life than the ways of the world, and that following you is better than chasing after selfish goals. Help them to take failure, not as a measure of their worth, but as a chance for a new start. Give them strength to hold their faith in you, and to keep alive their joy in your creation; through Jesus Christ our Lord. Amen (BCP, 829).

9 Adults in the Church Community in Need of Teaching and Learning

Introductory Meditations

On a journey, Jesus entered a village where a woman named Martha welcomed him to her home. She had a sister named Mary, who seated herself at the Lord's feet and listened to his words. Martha, who was busy with all the details of hospitality, came to him and said: "Lord are you not concerned that my sister has left me to do the household tasks all alone? Tell her to help me."

The Lord in reply said to her: "Martha, Martha, you are anxious and upset about many things; one thing only is required. Mary has chosen the better portion, and she shall not be deprived of it." (Adapted from Luke 10:38–42)

After entering Jericho, Jesus passed through the city. There was a man there named Zacchaeus, the chief tax collector and a wealthy man. He was trying to see what Jesus was like, but being small of stature, was unable to do so because of the crowd. He first ran on in front, then climbed a sycamore tree that was along Jesus' route in order to see him. When Jesus came to the spot, he looked up and said: "Zacchaeus, hurry down. I mean to stay at your house today." He quickly descended, and welcomed Jesus with delight. When this was observed, everyone began to murmur, "He has gone to a sinner's house as a guest." Zacchaeus stood his ground, and said to the Lord: "I give half my belongings, Lord, to the poor. If I have defrauded anyone in the least, I will pay him back fourfold." Jesus said to him: "Today salvation has come to this house, for this is what it means to be a son of Abraham. The Son of Man has come to search out and save what was lost." (Adapted from Luke 19:1–10)

I invite you to light a candle, preferably a scented candle, and spend some time looking at the flame and being aware of the scent of the candle or its light. If you have a scented candle, be aware of the smell, its sweetness, fragrance, and invisibility. As you look at the candle, be aware of how it burns quietly, as if giving of itself freely.

As you center or calm yourself, I invite you to read Luke 10:38–41. Place yourself at the feet of Jesus. Look at the feet, knees, stomach, hands, chest, lips, and eyes of Jesus. What do you like about Jesus? What do you like about what Jesus teaches you? What does Jesus say to you? What do you say to Jesus?

Now picture yourself in the classroom teaching. See if you can capture what is usually in your heart, mind, and soul as you teach, and try to imagine what is in the hearts, minds, and souls of the students who gather to listen to you on Sundays. Are your students happy to be there? Would your students rather be somewhere else? Why do they come to church school? Why do they stay away?

Remember that these meditations are tools to help you examine your life as a religious teacher and educator. It is important that you spend time looking at these questions and praying about them. A great way to ensure that you spend time with these questions is to write down your answers or write a poem or prayer in response to what you discover.

Adults in the Church Community in Need of Teaching and Learning

The story of Zaccheus is a perfect one to begin our discussion on the religious education of adults. Some time ago while visiting a parish, the teachers told me that they wanted to discuss a problem they were having with church school. I expected a problem with the curriculum, the teachers, or even the rector. Instead I heard a story that still baffles me. The teachers told me that a group of mothers would drop their kids off for church school, and instead of going into church, would stick around, coffee in hand, to listen to what was being said in church school. This made the teachers quite uncomfortable, because the parents were not going to church. In the story of Zaccheus, we see a man climbing up a tree to see Jesus, but in this church community, we see the adults doing anything to avoid seeing the rector.

As a teacher in the church, do I have the posture of Zaccheus? Do I want to see Jesus? How do I encourage others to see him?

As church communities we must never forget that the rector needs to learn and teach, and so does the congregation. When we talk about the universal priesthood of all believers, we own our equality before God while owning our need for God. In the same way that the church has a need for the ordained ministry, the church also has a need for teachers. We are all priests and teachers, but the church community must exercise its mission by calling priests for ordination and teachers for playing a special role in supporting others in their life in Christ. No parish can deny that all are in need of being taught, the vestry and clergy being no exception, but there is a strong need for specially prepared people to serve as teachers.

Discernment of the right time to call or invite the adult to a deeper experience of faith is a most important task for the church and its teachers. Often church communities leave the hesitant person in the tree, on the last bench, and on the fringes of community life. When the teachers told me about the coffee-drinking mothers, I asked whether anyone had pointed the parents to what was going on in church. There was no answer, only smiles. I left the question alone. Teachers must keep asking the question of how to attract adults to what they are doing.

I was talking to a priest some months ago. She told me that her parish was flourishing because she had started to offer courses on meditation, yoga, and massage. These teaching opportunities caused many of the older adults to leave the church. They made it known that the church was not the sort of place for "those types of activities and the kind of people attracted to those activities." The priest, though dismayed at their departure, was not daunted, and continued to open up the church as a gathering place for all who wanted a safe haven. As more people poured into the church and offered their suggestions, the priest realized that the seating in the church did not lend itself to active listening and participation. A few weeks later, I saw her in a bookstore. She was buying a book that explained how changing the church's seating could enhance how the message is heard. I thought to myself, now you will really alienate many within the church. But the priest seemed happy and unworried. She explained to me that many of those who had left had started returning to the church and had admitted to being frightened at first, but now were willing to face the need for changes. The priest was happy because she was a good teacher and knew how to invite people to look beyond themselves and toward new things.

Adult education of Christians within the church is just as important as the education of youth and children. An educational deficiency in any of these groups will deeply affect the life of the whole church. Religious education is a ministry that is intergenerational because all are in need of learning about their faith, the Bible, and what it means to live out their baptismal promises. It is especially important that those who teach children and youth make it their duty to receive ongoing Christian education themselves.

Quite frequently the debate on the place of children in the worshipping community tends to focus on whether children can understand the liturgy. I would put money down that most adults have no better understanding of the liturgy than do children. That is the case more and more because of what I call *adult dissatisfac-*

tion; adults go church shopping, and when they do settle, they need to gather a little more than religious moss. Adults need to receive education on what it means to have a relationship with Jesus, the Bible, ongoing conversion, the sacraments, and the ethics of Christian living. Just as important is the lesson of being part of a community of believers.

When I speak of religious education, I am talking about the process that draws out of the subject her or his growing understanding of the foundational issues and their effect on her or his daily life. Few adults get the chance to talk about their life of faith in a setting that welcomes their thoughts and offers them something more life-giving than pat answers—hope rooted in the mystery of Easter. Like the teachers of children and youth, special care must be made to call competent teachers to the ministry of adult education. These teachers must have not only knowledge of the church, faith, and the Bible, but healthy relationships with Jesus and others in the church.

In addition, those who teach adults in the church must appreciate the social, political, ethical, religious, and emotional dimensions of the human psyche, especially as those issues manifest themselves in adulthood. Oftentimes adults may be dealing with issues of addiction, loss, guilt, pain, and doubts that mere knowledge of the Bible or the church cannot address adequately. Though I do not believe that one needs a master's degree to teach, one should have broad knowledge that allows one to provide information or to humbly promise to research questions, as the case may be.

Zacchaeus was trying to see what Jesus was like. His desire led him into the crowds, through the crowds, away from the crowds, and into a tree. To be an adult is to make a journey to see what Jesus, life, children, religion, work, and job are like. A church community, especially one involved in education, has to commit itself to looking up into the trees, because the person looking for Jesus may be there.

Teachers and educators must practice looking in the right places at the right times. Teachers must find ways to lead the adult from theory into praxis that promotes justice and liberation, to lead the adult from looking down to looking within—and from looking within to looking with.

Adult formation or education is a process that leads the adult to a new place, by assuring the adult that the church desires to come and stay where the adult lives. As with the child and the youth, education then becomes a desire for the teachers and the church to find the adult *right where the adult is.*

Jesus goes to the home of Zacchaeus, suggesting to all those who educate within the church that religious education is always connected to the home. Religious education cannot take place in opposition to or disconnected from what happens in the home or the workplace. Though I do not advocate that teachers visit the job sites of those in their parishes, I do believe that what we teach in church should have an effect in the home and at work. What happens in the church gets lived out in terms of role modeling, servant-leadership style, conflict and resolution, making hard choices, personal responsibility, morale building, and many other behaviors that challenge the wider culture with values rooted in love and oriented toward the neighbor.

What Jesus does in the life of Zacchaeus is crucial to our understanding of our mission and ministry as teachers in the church. Jesus liberates Zacchaeus. Jesus touched him because Jesus was unafraid of the critics. Church teachers must be able to meet the adult in their despair, pride, stock options, cynicism, skepticism, doubt, depression, pretensions, and weaknesses. Let the critics talk all they want and talk what they want: what is important is that the teacher and the church value every adult.

When teachers meet adults and value them, they enable the adults to give freely of themselves. Enabling another person to give freely is allowing the person a chance to speak. The African method of Bible study and the method of dialogue employed in the base communities in South America are great ways of allowing adults to begin to feel comfortable about expressing their religious stirrings. Unfortunately our worship and the church community do not always make opportunities for adults to sit and talk about their lives with freedom. Doubts are not welcomed in our liturgy and worship. And when we pray and talk about weaknesses as adults, too often it is about another person, another's plight, and another's sins.

The two stories of Jesus valuing adults, in one case Mary, and in the other case Zacchaeus, show Jesus' level of comfort in different situations. To have someone sitting at your feet can be just as intimidating as having someone in a tree. To look down into the eyes of someone waiting at your feet or to look up at someone crouched in a tree can require courage. Jesus does it, and so must religious teachers. Teachers in the Christian tradition must know their own comfort level, push beyond it, lose themselves, and live in hope. Only then can they require the same thing of those they teach.

Christian education brings about conversion, brings about a righteousness and right living, often not immediately, but that is always the goal and the hope. Education is a lifelong process, and it is harmful for those in the church to take a short-sighted view.

> A young man came to a teacher and asked, "How long will it take me to attain wisdom and all the other gifts of the Spirit?"
>
> The teacher responded, "Seven years."
>
> The young man was clearly disturbed, "Seven years? That is quite a long time."
>
> "I am sorry," said the teacher, "Did I say seven years? I meant twelve years."
>
> Jumping up and down in disbelief, the man said, "What, are you crazy? What could require so much time? Not even a Ph.D. takes that long."
>
> The teacher replied, "You know, I think in your case it may well take forty years if you stayed with me, but other teachers would need at least fifty years."
>
> The young man walked away, and started telling the people in the village that the teacher had lost his marbles. The young man never returned to the teacher's house and village.

Teachers of adults need to pay special attention to the role that time plays in the life of adults and to how we view time. Many adults, like Martha, see time as the opportunity to do something productive. Adults value their time by showing what they produce and collecting a paycheck. In truth, most adults would prefer to earn more and work less, and many are caught up in the cultural business, an obsession with doing *stuff* all the time.

A popular warning these days remind us that we are *human beings, not human doings.* Most adults, I suspect, spend more time *doing* rather than *being.* Like Martha, they get frustrated when others relax, go on retreats, take vacations, or meditate when things *have* to be done. The things that have to be done have their place, of course. Jesus wanted to eat a meal, most likely wanted an environment that was clean, and wanted to feel comfortable. House cleaning does not happen by the grace of God. Work is important, but it is not the most important part of our lives.

Like religious education for youth and children, adult religious education requires some work. It must be well planned and provided at a suitable time when adults can come. Many churches get stuck on the idea that they have to provide religious education on Sundays, in one time slot, and only as a Bible study. Why not try a book club, a poetry club, religious paintings, and looking at religion from other perspectives? Try Wednesday night, try Thursday afternoon, and try Sunday night. We might be surprised at how many people find the time to come and to share their work and stories.

For the last few years, I have been promoting workshops for teachers on different methods of teaching. The attendance has been far from encouraging, though those who have attended claim to have found it worthwhile. A friend of mine said that a lot of what determines the attendance at workshops is the marketing and the prior research of needs. If people are just not interested in a certain topic, they won't come to listen to it. Another friend said: "No matter what you do, they won't come. People are just lazy, they want you to come to them." I suspect that there is no easy solution; one has to be willing to try different things, ways, and places for educational opportunities.

In our busy culture, part of the task of Christian education for life is to teach people how to waste time. Much has been said about the parable of the prodigal son and how the real message of the story is about the prodigal father. Indeed, a church community that educates for life has to find ways of encouraging members to be prodigal with their time.

Christians seem so willing to give their time for so many other things, but they grumble in irritation—or even resentment—if the liturgy runs five minutes overtime. Ever notice these days that there is no silence in church? It would be considered a waste of time. Every second in church is filled up with music, talking, and prayers. The liturgy has also lost the value of *wasting* time with God. All this supports my premise that education is for the whole people of God. All are in need of learning from Mary the value of sitting at the feet of Jesus and learning.

The young man in the preceding story wanted to know how long it would take him to gain wisdom. The parallel question of today's Christians might be whether they have to keep coming to church or to Christian education classes after obtaining some basic knowledge of the faith and liturgical practice. Those in charge of religious education can help adults recognize the ongoing need for time devoted to Christian learning.

This is a tough task, because most Christians believe that they are doing just fine and do not need anything the church has to offer beyond worship on Sunday mornings. A simple reference to or discussion of the baptismal vows or promises is one way of introducing the concept of a commitment to education that is necessarily ongoing. Or a simple question about how Christianity affects one's life. Sometimes people are not aware of the richness of their Christian faith and its value in their lives. We can hope that the whole church community can participate in sharing the benefits of Christian witness, in addition to pointing out the requirements and responsibilities of church membership.

To lead and to be led is the supreme path of education in the church and a clear manifestation of discipleship. Those who seek to lead adults should give them a chance to articulate their needs and desires. I do not suggest coming to adult sessions with prepackaged educational materials, but rather to be prepared to lead discussions, reflections, and thought processes through a crossroads of biblical, religious, and theological landscapes.

I was reviewing a curriculum the other day that had various stages from preschool to adult. I confess to having a special liking for this curriculum, and am not sure what made me look at it more closely. Surprisingly, the scriptural background information is the same for all levels. Those teaching children are given the same information as those teaching adults. I do not think this is appropriate, and that is why I call for those who work in the ministry of forming and educating adults to take the time to get the appropriate knowledge, information, and resources to work with adults.

In the same way, though homilies can serve for all generations, there have to be days when the language and content of the homily are geared toward only the children or only the youth. The needs of children, youth, and adults differ. God meets us in our needs and concerns and addresses them. Therefore God's message will vary depending on the understanding, the growth, and the development of the listener. The issues that a parent struggles with will be decidedly different from those of the child. Adults by their nature, or their time on earth, would normally have far more complicated experiences of life, love, betrayal, despair, and death.

Adult education or formation implies that the educational process and materials are more in depth and complex than those for children. This is not to presume that children and youth do not deal with complexities. But I maintain that there are differences in the stages of development, and I would be shocked if most people believed that in every situation, the message that is appropriate for the child would also work for the youth or the adult.

> Come, Spirit of God, and fill us with your love.
> Make us children who long for your Spirit and love.
> Come, Holy Spirit, walk with us with love.
> Give us youthful thoughts and hearts, and strength to live in love.
> Come, Everlasting Spirit, blowing in the depths and up above.
> Make us strong; may we know God's grace and live lives of love.
> Make us mature, childlike, and youthful, adults wanting more.
> Amen.

10 Teaching That Involves Death

Introductory Meditations

When Mary came to the place where Jesus was, seeing him, she fell at his feet and said to him, "Lord, if you had been here, my brother never would have died." When Jesus saw her weeping, and the Jews who had accompanied her also weeping, he was troubled in spirit, moved by the deepest emotions. "Where have you laid him?" he asked. "Lord, come and see," they said. Jesus began to weep, which caused the Jews to remark, "See how much he loved him!" But some said, "He opened the eyes of that blind man. Why could he not have done something to stop this man from dying?" Once again troubled in spirit, Jesus approached the tomb. (Adapted from John 11:32–38)

There is an appointed time for everything,
And a time for every affair under the heavens.
A time to be born, and a time to die;
A time to plant, and a time to uproot the plant;
A time to kill, and a time to heal;
A time to tear down, and a time to build;
A time to weep, and a time to laugh;
A time to mourn, and a time to dance;

     .   .   .   .

A time to rend, and a time to sew;
A time to be silent, and a time to speak;
A time to love, and a time to hate;
A time of war, and a time of peace.
(Adapted from Ecclesiastes 3:1–4,7–8)

121

Take a few minutes to reread the passage from John. Note the words or phrases that appeal to you. You might make a mental note of them or write them down. Try to keep it to no more than three words or phrases, or it might become too much of a task to remember them.

Calling to mind your first word or phrase, allow it to roll through your mind, and see if you can visualize the word or phrase, allowing it to massage the space you call your mind.

Now allow the word to rest in your heart. You may want to touch your heart as a way of reminding yourself to allow the word to dwell there. Spend some time with the word or phrase in your heart. Then ask the word to speak to your whole life, and see what happens. Take about ten minutes to do this exercise. Then come back to it at another time during the day or on another day.

Repeat the same exercise with the passage from Ecclesiastes.

If you work with children, I would encourage you to spend a lot of time with this question. See if you can get in touch with your childhood memories of death and suffering, and then think about your own children or children you know, and wonder what they think about suffering and death:

• As a child what were my views about death?
• What are my views on pain, suffering and death?
• What does God want to teach me about suffering and death?
• What are the things that cause me grief?
• Whose absence or death pains me the most?

I cannot overstate the importance of a teacher spending time reflecting on his or her own experience with pain, suffering, and death. You might have other ways of thinking about these questions. Feel free to use other Scripture passages for reflection, or you might want to reflect on a song or a poem. I hope that the time spent on this will reveal to you what God wants to teach you and what you can teach others about death.

Teaching That Involves Death

As I mentioned in section one, teaching must always include lessons on death. In the Christian community, to teach for life is to
teach the things that cause death and that help the Christian know
how to die well. In addition to reflecting together on how to live
and die, together we also profess as Christians to be *catholic;* common sense tells us that we are part of a global religious movement.
This can inspire us to teach our children, youth, and adults about
the reality of other Christians in the world, a reality that often includes facing death more often than it does for most of us in the
United States.

Here, then, is an opportunity to teach what it is like to be a
Christian in different circumstances, especially where Christians
die for their faith or die from hunger. Martyrdom has become quite
a common experience these days, and educators can draw out the
value of this gift that the church possesses through the faith of
others. People in Asia, Africa, and Latin America are dying for the
faith, dying because others do not live their faith, and dying because of the selfishness of many First World Christians.

If children, youth, and adults learn how to live well and die
well, life will take on a whole new meaning. All human beings face
death of some kind. How children accept and mourn death or loss
will be different from the youth and the adult. Church teachers
should find appropriate and age-specific ways to address questions of loss and death. What is important, however, is that the issues of death and loss are included in religious education. Good
Friday is one of the best times to talk about death, and I do not
mean in the homily, and I do not mean that death should be talked
about only on Good Friday.

The movie *Moonstruck* has a compelling scene in which a
wife wants to know why men cheat in relationships. The character
keeps asking people she meets, "Why do men cheat?" She receives
varied answers, and none of them satisfies her. Finally someone
says to her, "Men cheat because they are afraid of dying." Fear of
death and death itself affect how human beings live. Religious educators and teachers cannot miss out on one of the most important lessons for the Christian life.

When teachers teach about Jesus to children, youth, and adults, there must be overt references to the death of Jesus. Jesus struggled with death, accepted death, and ultimately gave himself up to death. Every Sunday in our various creeds we profess faith in Jesus who "died and was buried." Much of what Jesus preached stemmed from his awareness of the death he would have to face. I believe that Jesus feared death in a healthy way, because of how he lived. Jesus was too smart and too holy a man not to realize that his lifestyle would lead to death.

This becomes the lesson that Christian educators need to open up to children, youth, and adults. If Jesus knew that death was a reality because of how he chose to live, in obedience to God's love and vision for the world, how should Christians live? With our obsession about health these days, we know that many things will kill us or shorten our lives. It is not too much to ask that educators help members in the church examine their lives to address whether they are living well and living for Christ.

I believe that death is our most intimate and unrecognized partner in life. Death accompanies us every step of the way and in every aspect of life, but too often—and the church is especially guilty of this—we act as though death happens only in faraway countries and the moment when a person is placed in the coffin. Plants die, pets die, friends die, parents die, and many parts of our bodies die quietly and daily.

Having worked with immigrants, I realize how many of the adults face problems with depression, lack of health care, and worries about education and relationships. I wonder how many churches think about the masses of people who are slowly dying around them. As we speak of ourselves as being *catholic,* let us stop to think about the millions of Christians who are dying daily in war and unjust systems, fueled by Christian governments and their policies. Do we realize how many children die each minute because they have no food, no one to hold them, and no one to love them? Can we teach about Christ's love without recognizing that Christ still dies in our midst and around the world?

Many people would object to having to teach all this in religious education, but I do not think we can talk about life and the

Resurrection without touching on what the absence of life and the Resurrection mean. Holistic religious education looks at and addresses suffering because Jesus did. That the writers of the gospels included the slaughtering of the innocent, the plight of the Samaritans, the lepers, the children, the blind, and the lame shows us that they affected Jesus' ministry, and therefore should affect our living like Jesus.

Those who try to separate politics from religion do both politics and religion a disservice. Any teacher who teaches adults without addressing these issues fails to prepare the Christian to address the issues in today's world.

It is important to be global in our thinking and education. It is most important to allow the happenings from around the world to educate us, to lead us from beyond our world into a reality that accurately describes what it means to live as human beings in today's world.

At the same time, it is most important to keep it real, because too often we can focus on the outside and pay little attention to what is happening in our lives, our church, and our society. It becomes even more ridiculous when we lament the poverty and horrible situations in Third World countries and fail to realize the role Christianity and First World countries have played in ensuring that many of these countries will remain perpetually poor. To pray and work for justice in these countries is best done from a standpoint of knowledge and grace, and for this we need religious education.

As we stay real, focusing on life and death, adult educators must be aware of the things that cause death for the adults in their congregation. What are the local issues that cause stress, deny life, and cause pain? Somehow parishes, rectors, and lay educators have gotten stuck on the externals, forgetting that everybody suffers. How are adults given the space to talk about divorce, betrayals, and the effects of war, addiction, failings, sickness, and bankruptcy? How do adults know that there is a place for them and their concerns in church? How do adults learn that the Christian community has a philosophy and a lifestyle that can help on the journey and in the process of healing?

Our life process is fraught with learning, and because we are mortals, death forms an intimate part of that reality. Few parents who wait for the birth of a child do not reflect on the transitory nature of life. Women, in childbirth, have a deeper appreciation of pain and death. As a child grows, parents often think of the child's death. Most parents are not even aware of it, but most of their actions in relation to the child are to protect the child from harm, and ultimately from death.

Although we cannot protect ourselves and those we love from death, we can help them to learn positive things from the experiences of pain, suffering, and death. We cannot allow one of the central teachings of the Eucharist to escape us: our belief in the resurrection. To teach Christianity is to help Christians realize that death, pain, and all the things we fear never have the final word. Beyond death is the resurrection; beyond our addictions is a life that is worth living. To teach the resurrection is to teach hope when we as children, youth, and adults face despair, sorrow, fear, and death. All need to learn how to embrace and teach life and death.

In one of his most poignant and misunderstood teachings, Jesus says that unless a grain of wheat falls into the ground and dies, it still remains a grain of wheat. He also said that the person who tries to resist death will die, and those who embrace death will live. Adults have perfected the art of resisting and avoiding death. I suspect that fear has a huge part to play in their resistance to death, but I attribute education (bad education) as the second factor that leads to a denial of death among Christians and adults.

We can change that, and we must. Children, youth, and adults often remain selfish, frustrated, and disappointed in life because they have not learned the lessons about letting go, accepting suffering, or dying.

Evil, sin, and death must be part of every curriculum—not to be overemphasized but to serve as a reminder and a reality check of what it means to be human. Evil, sin, suffering, pain, and death are aspects of human life as much as joy, success, hope, grace, intelligence, and faith are. And so if we celebrate the positive things in life, we have to find ways of pointing to the not-so-positive, and challenge our children, youth, and adults to be part of the understanding or the solution.

Once a priest gave the most powerful and serious homily of her life. Even she felt the power of the Spirit as she delivered her words. She was teaching her congregation about death, how to die in the Lord, and the importance of living well. She closed her homily by repeating these words seven times, "Everybody who belongs to this church will die." When she finished her homily, she noticed that one man was laughing uncontrollably. During the exchange of peace, she asked him why he was laughing. "You said everybody in this congregation is going to die. I am so glad that I am only visiting."

As I said before, to teach well and to teach for life is to teach about death and its sting, because yes, the sting does exist, and it would be an injustice to pretend that there is no pain in the sting. Our education falls short if we do not proclaim that death and life form part of our experience as humans, and the greater of these is life.

11 Bathing in the River

We have discussed education on all levels—how it must be for life and across the board. We have looked briefly at some of the issues facing our children, youth, and adults in church and in society. We have spent a great deal of time meditating on our life lessons and some time thinking about our experience of pain and death. The Scripture passages have helped us focus on the responses of children, youth, and adults to God. I hope we feel more equipped as individuals to take our place with the wider church community in this process of education.

I now invite you to spend some time in meditation as a means of closing this section.

Find three pictures of yourself that represent three different stages in your life. You might choose one that represents your childhood, one your teen years, and one your adult years. Or choose any three pictures that represent changes or different stages in your life. Light a candle and place it before one of the pictures, preferably the picture of you as a child.

Invite Jesus or the Spirit to draw close to you, and try to be aware of God's presence. If the pictures and the candle get in the way, you can put them away, or you can do this meditation while walking.

Begin to pray about your life, first thanking the Lord for all the graces and blessings you received as a child. Then you may want to think about the times when you felt God's absence; see if you can hear

*yourself asking God why you felt alone in those moments. Stay with
this prayer (even for a few days) until you feel God's answer.*

*Repeat this exercise, concentrating on and praying about your expe-
rience as a youth and as an adult—or whatever stages of life you
choose. Then select one or two questions from the bulleted list below
and focus your attention on the issue raised as it relates to your experience in education.*

- Teaching for life is a commitment to a lifelong process of learning
  and asking questions about what it means to live as committed
  Christians. It involves a willingness to examine all aspects of life
  and how those areas affect our lives and those of other Christians in the world. To teach for life is to teach in a way that the
  child, youth, and adult grow in their appreciation of life and
  death?
    - *How are life and death manifested in my Christian life?*
- Baptism is the sacrament that brings us officially into a particular Christian family. As baptized Christians we profess a belief in
  Jesus Christ, who reveals the Spirit and the Creator God to us.
  We pledge in Baptism to put our "whole trust in his grace and
  love" (BCP, 302). Christian education, therefore, teaches us what
  it means to live as baptized Christians and how to live out a trust
  in God's grace and love in our relationships with others.
    - *What activities in my life manifest my trust in God's grace and
      love?*
- Children are full members of the church. Indeed, they best illustrate what it means to be Christlike. In our efforts to educate children, we have to open ourselves to learn from them. Children
  have something to teach us through their innocence, beauty,
  doubts, and rascality.
    - *How do I help children feel like full members of the church?*
- Part of our discussion has focused on going out to the margins to
  find the youth or going to the places where youth love to "hang
  out." Religious education allows youth to bring to the church and
  to those who teach them all the issues of life that excite and frus-
  trate youth. Those who teach youth must be committed to hear-

ing from them the things that place them on the margins of religious, social, and cultural life.

> • *What efforts do I make to learn about the religious, social, and cultural views of youth?*

• Adults are just as much in need of religious education as are children and youth. The issues that affect adults at an emotional, psychological, and spiritual level must be taken into account as part of the educational process. An important part of adult Christian education is to prepare them to take a more active part in the church's ministry and to help them provide role models for youth and children. Conversion, God's unconditional love, and the challenges of the Christian life are important elements in adult Christian education.

> • *How prepared am I to share my struggles with conversion and the challenges of the Christian life?*

• The church represents people gathered as the family of God. This is a reality that reminds us that we belong to many families, and that each family has its own set of obligations and responsibilities. Christian educators are committed to a healthy family life, and for this reason they support parents as primary educators of their children.

> • *As a religious teacher, how do I review my relationship with the parents or family members of those I teach?*

• As the body of Christ, we believe that we are a universal church. Being a universal church requires of us that we pray for and support our Christian and non-Christian brothers and sisters throughout the world.

> • *How do I foster a Christianity that is global and one that speaks to the injustices faced by many in this country and worldwide?*

• Death and sin are realities of our world, and the church community is not immune to their effects. Religious education cannot avoid teaching about the Christian response to these two realities. The message of hope, forgiveness, and the resurrection should form part of every Christian curriculum and be taught to all ages.

> • *How aware am I of the effects of sin, death, and pain in my life, and how have I experienced Jesus in those moments?*

- We have used many passages from the Bible to talk about the education of the child, youth, and adult. Most of the passages involve a discovery, a conversion, and a pursuit. In many ways they provide one aspect of the education process that continues for the rest of one's life.
  - *How do I share in God's work of discovery, conversion, and pursuit?*
- In section one I insisted on the need for teachers to have self-knowledge. In section two I explored the concept of self-knowledge by revisiting the stages in our lives when we were children, youth, and (young) adults.
  - *How does reflecting on my experiences as a child, a youth, and an adult affect my understanding of education?*

Ask yourself the following questions about each of the statements listed below: Am I effective? How can I improve? Where can I find help in this area? How can the church support me?

- A teacher is called to grow in wisdom.
- A teacher is called to be a companion on the journey.
- A teacher is called to be a prophet.
- A teacher is called to be a storyteller.
- A teacher is called to be a healer.
- A teacher is called to be an inventor.
- A teacher is called to live the truth.
- A teacher is called to respect all persons.
- A teacher is called to be a welcoming presence.
- A teacher is called to be a disciple of Christ.

III

The Family
Living and Teaching Christianity

12 Day by Day along the Way, the Family Stays Together

Introductory Meditations

To begin this section, I would like to suggest that we spend some time reflecting on what it means to live and teach Christianity as members of a family.

- What are the most frequently asked religious questions in my family?
- What questions would I like to ask my family about God?
- How, when, where, and why do we pray as a family?
- What joyful event has brought us closer to God?
- What tragic event has distanced us from God?
- What is my family's experience of Sunday worship?
- Does God or can God make a difference in my family life?

Read the following passage slowly one or two times. Read three or four words and keep them in mind, listen to your breathing, then read a few more words, continuing this process until you finish reading the whole passage.

When the day came to purify them according to the law of Moses, the couple brought him up to Jerusalem so that he could be presented to the Lord . . . and when the parents brought in the child Jesus, to perform for him the customary ritual of the law, Simeon took him in his arms and praised God. . . . The child's father and mother were marveling at what was being said about him. Simeon blessed them and said to Mary, his mother: "This child is destined to be the downfall and the rising up of many in

Israel, a sign that will be opposed, and your own soul will be pierced with a sword—and the thoughts of many hearts will be laid bare." (Adapted from Luke 2:22–35)

Much of Christianity is defined as a following of Jesus—a journeying with and a presentation of Jesus; some of us follow without remembering why we are following. We often become individualistic about our following of Jesus, and forget the importance of worshipping as a family. I invite you to spend some time rediscovering what makes you follow Jesus and what importance God has for your family. Here are a few questions that may aid your prayer time.

- When does my family pray together?
- How do I evaluate my family's relationship with Jesus?
- Why would I encourage other family members to live a Christian life?
- What does it mean for my family to be Christians?
- What does it mean for me to teach about Christ and to learn about Christ in my family?

I now invite you to spend some time with this prayer for families and the previous passage from Scripture.

All praise and thanks to you, most merciful Father, for adopting us as your own children, for incorporating us into your holy Church, and for making us worthy to share in the inheritance of the saints in light; through Jesus Christ your Son our Lord, who lives and reigns with you and the Holy Spirit, one God, for ever and ever. Amen (BCP, 311).

Day by Day along the Way, the Family Stays Together

The more time I spend with church-school teachers, the more I hear how frustrated they are with parents who believe that religious education takes place only in the church. I want to dedicate the next few pages to parents of children and youth who may be at a loss as to how to assume their religious obligation to bring up their children as Christians.

For whatever reasons, parents find it difficult to see themselves as teachers. Parents teach their children the basics of life, the foundation of life, and the most important things in life, but when it comes to religious education, parents feel inadequate. My hope is that one day parents will feel confident enough to encourage religious learning in the home. The first step, I imagine, is for parents to recognize the innate presence of God in the young child.

When the child is in the home, God is in the home. Parents, I believe, have an innate temptation to bring their children to church or to school for the children to receive formation; but the time has come for parents to assume the primary responsibility for religious education. Parents cannot expect religious formation to happen only on Sundays in the parish.

A friend of mine, Helen Netos, in discussing the lack of religious formation in families, said she believes that parents feel unprepared to discuss salvation history. They do not know how to begin an articulation of their faith. Parents know that they are Christians, believing people, and the people of God, but they are not comfortable putting it into words. Those who work in religious formation have to make it clear to parents that words pale in comparison to actions. To paraphrase a popular saying, "The unlived Christian life is not worth teaching."

But what do parents need to know in order to participate in the religious formation of their sons and daughters? I want to suggest seven areas of religious education that might be worth exploring by parents. Why do I choose seven? Because there are seven days in a week, and parents may find it worthwhile to come back to each point as a new week begins. Creation-liberation, individuation-incarnation, negation-invitation, actualization-salvation, crucifixion-resurrection, articulation-education, and preparation-celebration are the seven pillars of Christian history. I believe this is the best outline of salvation history, and I hope to address each as a way of suggesting how parents, and teachers too, can approach teaching in the home.

Sunday During Pentecost or Ordinary Time (creation-resurrection)

We believe that God created. We believe that we belong to God. As the author of life, God holds all that we do and are in view. Life teaches us that many forces in our hearts and lives are opposed to life. Sin and death affect us as human beings and cause us to suffer pain and feel sad. But as Christians we also believe in the resurrection; we believe that life is stronger than death. Each Sunday we would do well to call to mind the mysteries of creation and resurrection.

Silence: *Invite family members to be quiet for a few minutes. So much of our day is surrounded by noise, so a few moments of silence go a long way. The goal of the silence is to grow in awareness of God's love and presence.*

Creation-resurrection question of the day: What do the words *creation* and *resurrection* mean to me? What importance do they hold for my life today? *Allow a few moments for people to share.*

Lectio Divina: *Family members should be encouraged to hear the word of God as desirous of taking up residence in their hearts. The reading should be done slowly, and there is no need to read the whole selection; at times it is better to repeat one verse several times. Choose one of the following passages:*
Genesis 2:1–25, Genesis 8:15–22, Psalm 67, Psalm 100, Psalm 150, Matthew 5:1–16, Luke 24:36–49

Meditatio: *This moment requires that we allow the word of God to enter more deeply into our minds. We spend time thinking about the word of God, and we isolate a word or phrase that helps us feel closer to God. Reading is like a potter preparing the clay; meditating is taking the clay and beginning to fashion it.*

An appointed person explains to the gathering that there will be another period of silence and that people are encouraged to visualize one of the following points of meditation:

• Be still for a few moments. Then imagine that you are at the Baptism of Jesus or the Pentecost event and that the Holy Spirit descends on you in the form of a tongue of fire or a dove. Feel the presence of the heavenly being on your head, and feel the heat radiate through your entire body, descending especially to your heart.
• Close your eyes and imagine that you are in God's hand being formed. Stay with this image, and experience what it must feel like to be created by God. If your mind strays, gently return to this image.
• Close your eyes and imagine that you are in the presence of Jesus on that first Easter morning. Stay with this image, and experience what it must feel like to be in the presence of the Risen Lord. Try to experience the joy of the Risen Lord. If your mind strays, gently return to the face of Jesus.
• Close your eyes and imagine that you are sitting next to Jesus, leaning on him. Imagine that you hear him repeat over and over again, "You are my child, I love you!"
• Close your eyes and think of all the beautiful things God has created. Hear God's voice saying, "You are good, I love you."
• Draw a picture or write a poem to express your feelings toward God.

Oratio: *This moment offers the opportunity to respond to God with thoughts or words of adoration, confessions, thanksgiving, and prayers for any aspect of your life that God may be calling you to change.*

Parents: Let us thank God for the good things we have. *(Silence or vocalized prayers)*
Children: Let us ask God's mercy for the times we have offended God and made each other sad. *(Silence or vocalized prayers)*
Parents: Let us bless God for the gift of love and all we are called to be. *(Silence or vocalized prayers)*
Children: Let us ask God to fill us with new life. *(Silence or vocalized prayers)*

Parents: God is good.
Children: All the time. All the time.
Parents: God is good.

Contemplatio: *This is another moment of silence. It is an important moment to notice what is happening in your heart and to further dedicate yourself to God. Use this moment to examine and appreciate all that has happened during this time of prayer.*

Parents or children: Let us be still for a brief moment and remind ourselves of what God has said to us in Scripture and in our thoughts.

Grace Resolve: *Family members can express a desire (or not) to try to do something for the Lord today, tomorrow, next week, or whenever possible.*

Monday (individuation-incarnation)

We encounter God as individuals. Our experiences as human beings help us to see God's activities in our life. To see God working in our lives and being born in our hearts are not easy tasks. Nor is growing into who God wants us to be and who we want to be. We can take much comfort in the Incarnation: Jesus became one of us and lived and died on earth. God loves us as we are. God loves us individually. God wants us to know that the incarnation continues in us, even as we individuate. So as we journey to find ourselves, let us ask Jesus, who knows what it is to be human, to teach us what it means to live holy lives.

Silence: *Invite family members to be quiet for a few minutes. So much of our day is surrounded by noise, so a few moments of silence go a long way. The goal of the silence is to grow in awareness of God's love and presence.*

Individuation-incarnation question of the day: What do both of these words mean to me? What importance do they hold for my life today? *Allow a few moments for people to share.*

Lectio Divina: *Family members should be encouraged to hear the word of God as desirous of taking up residence in their hearts. The reading should be done slowly, and there is no need to read the whole selection; at times it is better to repeat one verse several times. Choose one of the following passages:*
Genesis 12:1–9, Exodus 20:1–17, Psalm 23, Psalm 31, Psalm 62, Matthew 1:18–24, John 14:1–7

Meditatio: *This moment requires that we allow the word of God to enter more deeply into our minds. We spend time thinking about the word of God, and we isolate a word or phrase that helps us feel closer to God. Reading is like a potter preparing the clay; meditating is taking the clay and beginning to fashion it.*

An appointed person explains to the gathering that there will be another period of silence and that people are encouraged to visualize one of the following points of meditation:

- Try to sit still and calm yourself. Be aware of your breathing, and imagine that the breath of God is being breathed through you. Repeat these words in your heart, "Jesus, Son of the living God, have mercy on me." Do not try to fight your thoughts, but as often as you can, return to this prayer, "Jesus, Son of the living God, have mercy on me."
- Close your eyes and try to be still. Imagine that God is holding you. Use your imagination to see how you are being held by God. Feel what it is like to be held by someone who loves you. Imagine that you hear God saying to you softly, "I have loved you with an everlasting love; nothing can separate you from me." Without losing the sense that you are being held by God, keep coming back to these words.
- Sit with your hands open and on your knees. Close your eyes and imagine that you are sitting in your favorite spot. Try to be as comfortable as possible. As you sit there, imagine that Jesus is calling you by name. Respond to Jesus by saying, "Here I am." Spend a few moments listening for what Jesus may be asking of you. Feel free to keep repeating, "Here I am" or "Speak, Lord, I am listening."

- Close your eyes and think of two of the most important moments in your life. What was God's reaction at the time? What is God's reaction now? Slowly repeat to Jesus, "Thank you for always being with me."
- Be still and think of your favorite song. Imagine Jesus singing this song with you or for you. You might even return the favor: have Jesus sit in your favorite chair and then sing to Jesus.
- Draw a picture or write a poem to express your feelings toward God.

Oratio: *This moment offers the opportunity to respond to God with thoughts or words of adoration, confessions, thanksgiving, and prayers for any aspect of your life that God may be calling you to change.*

Parents: Let us thank God for the good things we have. *(Silence or vocalized prayers)*
Children: Let us ask God's mercy for the times we have offended God and made each other sad. *(Silence or vocalized prayers)*
Parents: Let us bless God for the gift of love and all we are called to be. *(Silence or vocalized prayers)*
Children: Let us ask God to fill us with new life. *(Silence or vocalized prayers)*
Parents: God is good.
Children: All the time. All the time.
Parents: God is good.

Contemplatio: *This is another moment of silence. It is an important moment to notice what is happening in your heart and to further dedicate yourself to God. Use this moment to examine and appreciate all that has happened during this time of prayer.*

Parents or children: Let us be still for a brief moment and remind ourselves of what God has said to us in Scripture and in our thoughts.

Grace Resolve: *Family members can express a desire (or not) to try to do something for the Lord today, tomorrow, next week, or whenever possible.*

Tuesday (negation-invitation)

Many of us are afraid of loss, pain, and death. Yet, the best way to live is to face those challenges head on. We lose things every second, and the Scriptures call us to let go and "die to ourselves." Every experience of negation holds an invitation to deeper life. John the Baptist said that he needed to decrease so that Jesus could increase. Negation sometimes involves a lot of sacrifices, and sacrifices by their nature can be painful. It is a great grace to reflect on how life, our friends, and God call and challenge us to let go and let God. Whenever we feel small, negated, or lost, it is important to know that God is calling us to new life and hope.

Silence: *Invite family members to be quiet for a few minutes. So much of our day is surrounded by noise, so a few moments of silence go a long way. The goal of the silence is to grow in awareness of God's love and presence.*

Negation-invitation question of the day: What do these words mean to me? What importance do they hold for my life today? *Allow a few moments for people to share.*

Lectio Divina: *Family members should be encouraged to hear the word of God as desirous of taking up residence in their hearts. The reading should be done slowly, and there is no need to read the whole selection; at times it is better to repeat one verse several times. Choose one of the following passages:*
Exodus 17:1–7, 1 Samuel 3:1–10, Psalm 122, Psalm 124, Luke 10:25–37, John 3:1–16, 1 Peter 2:1–10

Meditatio: *This moment requires that we allow the word of God to enter more deeply into our minds. We spend time thinking about the word of God, and we isolate a word or phrase that helps us feel closer to God. Reading is like a potter preparing the clay; meditating is taking the clay and beginning to fashion it.*

An appointed person explains to the gathering that there will be another period of silence and that people are encouraged to visualize one of the following points of meditation:

- Close your eyes and relax. Imagine that you are in church alone, it is evening, and there is just a candle burning in the church. Imagine that the light of the candle is making a path to your heart. See if you can hear Jesus saying, "You are my light to the world."
- Be still for a few moments. Imagine that you were a piece of Jesus' garment or a part of Jesus' body. Which piece of his garment or part of his body would you choose to be? Just be aware of what it means to be so close to Jesus.
- Say in a soft voice, "God loves me so much, that God gave me Jesus." Repeat this over and over. Slowly allow your heart to say these words in silence. Listen to your heart. Now imagine that you were saying it to the world, "God loves the world so much that God gave us Jesus."
- Sit as comfortably as you can. Imagine that you are walking through a desert. Imagine that you meet Jesus, and he offers you water and promises to stay with you for the rest of the journey. Choose a way of saying thanks to Jesus.
- Try to think of someone who is feeling lonely, sad, or depressed. Hear Jesus inviting you to be a source of joy for that person. Say to Jesus, "Lord, teach me to do your will." Repeat this a few times.
- Draw a picture or write a poem to express your feelings toward God.

Oratio: *This moment offers the opportunity to respond to God with thoughts or words of adoration, confessions, thanksgiving, and prayers for any aspect of your life that God may be calling you to change.*

Parents: Let us thank God for the good things we have. *(Silence or vocalized prayers)*
Children: Let us ask God's mercy for the times we have offended God and made each other sad. *(Silence or vocalized prayers)*
Parents: Let us bless God for the gift of love and all we are called to be. *(Silence or vocalized prayers)*
Children: Let us ask God to fill us with new life. *(Silence or vocalized prayers)*
Parents: God is good.
Children: All the time. All the time.
Parents: God is good.

Contemplatio: *This is another moment of silence. It is an important moment to notice what is happening in your heart and to further dedicate yourself to God. Use this moment to examine and appreciate all that has happened during this time of prayer.*

Parents or children: Let us be still for a brief moment and remind ourselves of what God has said to us in Scripture and in our thoughts.

Grace Resolve: *Family members can express a desire (or not) to try to do something for the Lord today, tomorrow, next week, or whenever possible.*

Wednesday (actualization-salvation)

Our human existence involves a committed search to find meaning and hope. As we search for meaning, love, hope, and God, we also search to be real. It is a human dream to be real, to be true, and to fulfill our dreams. "What does it mean to be me?" is just as important a question as "What does it mean to be real?" As we discover who we are and live out our dreams, we find God offering us salvation along the way. It is good to know that we are saved and are being saved by God. Part of our work as Christians is to live into the hope of salvation and to live lives as faithful disciples. We are called by God to be the children of God in a world that needs Christians who preach and live the Gospels.

Silence: *Invite family members to be quiet for a few minutes. So much of our day is surrounded by noise, so a few moments of silence go a long way. The goal of the silence is to grow in awareness of God's love and presence.*

Actualization-salvation question of the day: What do these words mean to me? What importance do they hold for my life today? *Allow a few moments for people to share.*

Lectio Divina: *Family members should be encouraged to hear the word of God as desirous of taking up residence in their hearts. The reading should be done slowly, and there is no need to read the whole selection; at times it is better to repeat one verse several*

times. Choose one of the following passages:
Exodus 13:1–10, 2 Kings 5:1–15, Psalm 1, Psalm 8, Matthew 6:25–33, Mark 14: 32–42, Romans 8:14–17

Meditatio: *This moment requires that we allow the word of God to enter more deeply into our minds. We spend time thinking about the word of God, and we isolate a word or phrase that helps us feel closer to God. Reading is like a potter preparing the clay; meditating is taking the clay and beginning to fashion it.*

An appointed person explains to the gathering that there will be another period of silence and that people are encouraged to visualize one of the following points of meditation:

- Imagine that you are sitting under a tree, next to a river. The sun is shining brightly, and you can feel its warmth on your skin. Imagine that the warmth is telling you that God loves you warmly and that the river is singing to you of God's love. Just sit under the tree and be aware of God's saving love.
- Close your eyes and relax. Imagine that you are standing next to the cross of Jesus. Imagine that you are there with Mary and John. Try to look at the face of Jesus, and ask him if there is anything you can do for him. Stay at the foot of the cross and listen for an answer.
- Imagine that you met Jesus on your way to school or work. Picture Jesus sitting next to you in the car, at school, or in your workplace. Ask Jesus, "What must I do to be saved?" Notice how Jesus responds.
- Sitting comfortably and with eyes closed, settle briefly and repeat the phrase "Lord, I believe, help my unbelief." Or you might want to say these words: "Lord save me, or I will perish." When you are finished, give thanks to God for saving you.
- Think of someone who is hurt, worried, or in need of a friend. Then think of Jesus hugging that person. Keep that image in mind, and pray that Jesus will heal or bless that person.
- Draw a picture or write a poem to express your feelings toward God.

Oratio: *This moment offers the opportunity to respond to God with thoughts or words of adoration, confessions, thanksgiving, and prayers for any aspect of your life that God may be calling you to change.*

Parents: Let us thank God for the good things we have. *(Silence or vocalized prayers)*
Children: Let us ask God's mercy for the times we have offended God and made each other sad. *(Silence or vocalized prayers)*
Parents: Let us bless God for the gift of love and all we are called to be. *(Silence or vocalized prayers)*
Children: Let us ask God to fill us with new life. *(Silence or vocalized prayers)*
Parents: God is good.
Children: All the time. All the time.
Parents: God is good.

Contemplatio: *This is another moment of silence. It is an important moment to notice what is happening in your heart and to further dedicate yourself to God. Use this moment to examine and appreciate all that has happened during this time of prayer.*

Parents or children: Let us be still for a brief moment and remind ourselves of what God has said to us in Scripture and in our thoughts.

Grace Resolve: *Family members can express a desire (or not) to try to do something for the Lord today, tomorrow, next week, or whenever possible.*

Thursday (articulation-education)

"Who am I?" This is the eternal question, and it requires over and over again that we answer it. Who I am as a Christian or a member of a religious group requires ongoing articulation. Articulation is more than professing. It means a commitment to ongoing learning and a desire to strive to live out one's Christian beliefs. The Apostles' Creed is one articulation of the Christian faith, but each Christian is called on a daily basis to articulate what it means to follow Jesus. Part of our articulation is education, and we must commit to Bible study and to individual and communal prayer. An educated Christian life is not worth articulating.

Silence: *Invite family members to be quiet for a few minutes. So much of our day is surrounded by noise, so a few moments of silence go a long way. The goal of the silence is to grow in awareness of God's love and presence.*

Articulation-education question of the day: What do either or both of these words mean to me? What importance do they hold for my life today? *Allow a few moments for people to share.*

Lectio Divina: *Family members should be encouraged to hear the word of God as desirous of taking up residence in their hearts. The reading should be done slowly, and there is no need to read the whole selection; at times it is better to repeat one verse several times. Choose one of the following passages:*
Exodus 3:1–8, Job 42:1–6, Psalm 95, Proverbs 1:8–15, Luke 9:23–27, John 10:1–10, Acts 9:1–9

Meditatio: *This moment requires that we allow the word of God to enter more deeply into our minds. We spend time thinking about the word of God, and we isolate a word or phrase that helps us feel closer to God. Reading is like a potter preparing the clay; meditating is taking the clay and beginning to fashion it.*
An appointed person explains to the gathering that there will be another period of silence and that people are encouraged to visualize one of the following points of meditation:

- Sit as comfortably as you can and close your eyes. Imagine that Jesus is standing before you and asking you, "What do you want me to do for you?" Speak to Jesus about your need, and then thank him for listening to you.
- Close your eyes and relax. Ask Jesus to teach you how to pray. Then try to be still for a few moments, and slowly repeat the Lord's Prayer. You might want to just keep repeating the prayer that Jesus taught, each time spending a longer period of time on

the words you like.
- Try to remember an incident in your life in which it was obvious to you that God was teaching you something. Ask God for the grace to help you live what you learned from that moment of grace.
- Imagine that Jesus stands before you with his hands extended. He is asking you to put your worries and concerns into his hands. Go toward Jesus and hand over to him whatever has been troubling you.
- Be still for a few moments. Spend some time thanking God for the blessings in your life. Ask God for the grace to be a sign of love for others.
- Draw a picture or write a poem to express your feelings toward God.

Oratio: *This moment offers the opportunity to respond to God with thoughts or words of adoration, confessions, thanksgiving, and prayers for any aspect of your life that God may be calling you to change.*

Parents: Let us thank God for the good things we have. *(Silence or vocalized prayers)*
Children: Let us ask God's mercy for the times we have offended God and made each other sad. *(Silence or vocalized prayers)*
Parents: Let us bless God for the gift of love and all we are called to be. *(Silence or vocalized prayers)*
Children: Let us ask God to fill us with new life. *(Silence or vocalized prayers)*
Parents: God is good.
Children: All the time. All the time.
Parents: God is good.

Contemplatio: *This is another moment of silence. It is an important moment to notice what is happening in your heart and to further dedicate yourself to God. Use this moment to examine and appreciate all that has happened during this time of prayer.*

Parents or children: Let us be still for a brief moment and remind ourselves of what God has said to us in Scripture and in our thoughts.

Grace Resolve: *Family members can express a desire (or not) to try to do something for the Lord today, tomorrow, next week, or whenever possible.*

Friday (crucifixion-liberation)

Every so often someone mentions the scandal of the cross. We can forget that we worship Jesus who was assassinated. Jesus died because he was true to God's will for his life and preached a Gospel of love and radical inclusion. We all feel crucified from time to time, and so do others. As we think about Christ's Crucifixion, we should call to mind the many who continue to be killed in our world. Sometimes the most difficult crucifixion is the one that takes place in our hearts and habits. We cringe from making the hard choices we need to make. For those who suffer unjustly, God will liberate them. God will liberate us in the moments when we feel crucified and face death.

Silence: *Invite family members to be quiet for a few minutes. So much of our day is surrounded by noise, so a few moments of silence go a long way. The goal of the silence is to grow in awareness of God's love and presence.*

Crucifixion-liberation question of the day: What do these words mean to me? What importance do they hold for my life today? *Allow a few moments for people to share.*

Lectio Divina: *Family members should be encouraged to hear the word of God as desirous of taking up residence in their hearts. The reading should be done slowly, and there is no need to read the whole selection; at times it is better to repeat one verse several times. Choose one of the following passages:*
Genesis 3:1–13, Exodus 3:1–8, Psalm 51, Psalm 74, Isaiah 42:1–8, Matthew 5: 43–48, Mark 8:31–38

Meditatio: *This moment requires that we allow the word of God to enter more deeply into our minds. We spend time thinking about the word of God, and we isolate a word or phrase that helps us feel* *closer to God. Reading is like a potter preparing the clay; meditating is taking the clay and beginning to fashion it.*

An appointed person explains to the gathering that there will be another period of silence and that people are encouraged to visualize one of the following points of meditation:

- Imagine that you are sitting with the disciples at the Last Supper. As Jesus says the words "This is my body, this is my blood," look into his eyes. Notice the expression on his face and notice your feelings for him.
- Be still and slowly repeat these words: "Christ has died. Christ is risen. Christ will come again." Invite the Holy Spirit to come anew into your heart.
- Sit as comfortably as you can. Imagine that you are the lost sheep. Picture yourself walking alone over mountains and through valleys. Get in touch with a feeling of being lost. Be aware that Jesus is coming to find you. Notice what it feels like to be alone as night falls and to be found by Jesus.
- Try to have no thoughts for a few moments. If your mind wanders, come back to the silence and a blank state of mind.
- Think of people who are in pain. Think of prisoners, sick people, and those who are hungry. Pray and ask God to be present to them.
- Draw a picture or write a poem to express your feelings toward God.

Oratio: *This moment offers the opportunity to respond to God with thoughts or words of adoration, confessions, thanksgiving, and prayers for any aspect of your life that God may be calling you to change.*

Parents: Let us thank God for the good things we have. *(Silence or vocalized prayers)*
Children: Let us ask God's mercy for the times we have offended God and made each other sad. *(Silence or vocalized prayers)*
Parents: Let us bless God for the gift of love and all we are called to be. *(Silence or vocalized prayers)*
Children: Let us ask God to fill us with new life. *(Silence or vocalized prayers)*

Parents: God is good.
Children: All the time. All the time.
Parents: God is good.

Contemplatio: *This is another moment of silence. It is an important moment to notice what is happening in your heart and to further dedicate yourself to God. Use this moment to examine and appreciate all that has happened during this time of prayer.*

Parents or children: Let us be still for a brief moment and remind ourselves of what God has said to us in Scripture and in our thoughts.

Grace Resolve: *Family members can express a desire (or not) to try to do something for the Lord today, tomorrow, next week, or whenever possible.*

Saturday (preparation-celebration)

Our Jewish brothers and sisters celebrate the Sabbath on this day. It is a day of rest for them, a time when they ponder what it is to be like God. For many Jews the Sabbath is a chance to imitate God by resting. When we rest, we renovate and rejuvenate. When we rest, we have a chance to prepare our hearts to meet God. As Christians we celebrate the Lord's Day on Sunday; how good it would be if we spent some time preparing for our worship experience. How do we prepare ourselves to celebrate our life in God? How do we prepare to meet God, not just in each other or on Sunday but also at the end of time?

Silence: *Invite family members to be quiet for a few minutes. So much of our day is surrounded by noise, so a few moments of silence go a long way. The goal of the silence is to grow in awareness of God's love and presence.*

Preparation-celebration question of the day: What do these words mean to me? What importance do they hold for my life today? *Allow a few moments for people to share.*

Lectio Divina: *Family members should be encouraged to hear the word of God as desirous of taking up residence in their hearts. The reading should be done slowly, and there is no need to read the whole selection; at times it is better to repeat one verse several times. Choose one of the following passages:*
Exodus 12:1–20, Deuteronomy 5:6–21, Psalm 66, Psalm 137, Luke 2:22–35, Luke 2:39–56, John 8:1–11

Meditatio: *This moment requires that we allow the word of God to enter more deeply into our minds. We spend time thinking about the word of God, and we isolate a word or phrase that helps us feel closer to God. Reading is like a potter preparing the clay; meditating is taking the clay and beginning to fashion it.*

An appointed person explains to the gathering that there will be another period of silence and that people are encouraged to visualize one of the following points of meditation:

- Be still and think of your favorite religious hymn. Allow the words to flow through your mind, and use them as a means of talking to Jesus.
- Imagine that you are at home alone and Jesus comes to visit you. What do you serve him? What do you talk about? How do you say good-bye when it is time for him to leave?
- Think of your favorite Bible passage, or a biblical healing story. Be one of the characters, and see what this teaches you about God's love, mercy, or healing.
- Close your eyes and imagine that you are a seagull or an eagle flying way up in the sky. Look down on the earth, and notice the beauty of the clouds and the trees. Imagine that the Holy Spirit joins you in your flight. Fly with the Holy Spirit. What does the Holy Spirit feel about the people and things on the earth?
- Be still and invite Jesus to come into your heart. Imagine that Jesus is baptizing you in the River Jordan. Feel the water running down your body, and feel his hands on your shoulder. Now imagine that the Holy Spirit descends on you. Hear the voice of God say, "This is my beloved child."
- Draw a picture or write a poem to express your feelings toward God.

Oratio: *This moment offers the opportunity to respond to God with thoughts or words of adoration, confessions, thanksgiving, and prayers for any aspect of your life that God may be calling you to change.*

Parents: Let us thank God for the good things we have. *(Silence or vocalized prayers)*
Children: Let us ask God's mercy for the times we have offended God and made each other sad. *(Silence or vocalized prayers)*
Parents: Let us bless God for the gift of love and all we are called to be. *(Silence or vocalized prayers)*
Children: Let us ask God to fill us with new life. *(Silence or vocalized prayers)*
Parents: God is good.
Children: All the time. All the time.
Parents: God is good.

Contemplatio: *This is another moment of silence. It is an important moment to notice what is happening in your heart and to further dedicate yourself to God. Use this moment to examine and appreciate all that has happened during this time of prayer.*

Parents or children: Let us be still for a brief moment and remind ourselves of what God has said to us in Scripture and in our thoughts.

Grace Resolve: *Family members can express a desire (or not) to try to do something for the Lord today, tomorrow, next week, or whenever possible.*

> And pointing to his disciples, he said, "Here are my mother and my brothers! For whoever does the will of my Father in heaven is my brother and sister and mother." (Matthew 12:49–50)

13 Finding God in All Things

Mom, is God everywhere? Is he between my toes? Is God in a rock?
Can God turn a square into a triangle and have it still be a triangle?

There are as many ways of finding and encountering God as there
are grains of sand on the seashore and stars in the heavens. All of
us experience God in different ways, events, things, and persons.
It has become widely known through work on multiple intelli-
gences that families and groups need to keep in mind that there
are different ways of meeting God and processing those experiences. There are multiple ways of finding God in and among multiple things.

A Way of Praying with Things
Anything can be used as a holy object. I have listed a few ideas
below, but you may have other things in which you can find God.

- Sit in silence for a few moments.
- Choose an object that you want to focus on in prayer.
- Sit comfortably and with your eyes closed.
- First, thank God for the gift of the object (see the object as gift).
- Think of how the object reminds you of God.
- Choose a holy word to go along with your object. For instance, if
  your object is a rock, you may think of strength.
- Make a prayer by saying, "Jesus, you are my *strength*." Repeat
  this line slowly.
- At the end of the prayer period, sit with your eyes closed for a
  few moments; then say the Our Father.

A few things . . .

Body Prayer: Stand, sit, or lie down. Thank God for the gift of your body. You might thank God for the gift of health, and if you are sick or in pain, gently touch the spot where you are sick, and repeat, "Jesus, the great physician, heal me." Another way of praying with the body is to stand and repeat: "This is holy ground. I am standing on holy ground because the Lord is here, and where God is, it is holy." Another way to pray with the body is to extend the arms and make your body into the shape of a cross. Talk to Jesus as if you were on a cross next to or before him. Making the sign of the cross over different parts of the body is another powerful way of remembering that our bodies are holy. How does your body remind you of God?

Think of a family member; it may be a person you love the most or the least. What are the qualities you admire in this person? What are the qualities that you don't like in this person? Bring the person's face to mind, and thank God for the gifts the person has. Then lovingly ask God to be present to the person in his or her weakness. How does this person remind you of God? How does this person help you in your life of faith?

Find an object in the house that you love, and spend ten minutes thinking about why you love that particular thing. Who gave it to you? If you bought it, why did you buy it? How does it remind you of God's love? Do you consider it holy? How does the object remind you of God?

Notice an object in the house that is simply useful rather than treasured. It may be the television, the refrigerator, a sofa, or a lamp. Think about how this object is used in the house. What would life in the house be like without it? Think about your role in the family? What object would you be? How does this object remind you of God?

The next time you get the chance, look at a tree. Look at it long enough so that later when you go to pray, you will have the image in your head. Where do the roots go? How does the tree stay alive? Does the tree provide fruit, beauty, or shade? How does the tree remind you of God? If possible, get a leaf, and pay attention to the leaf throughout the day. Repeat the same exercise for the leaf.

Look at the sky and notice the clouds, the sun, the stars, or the moon. What do you like about any of these? What purposes do they serve? What would life be like without them? Thank God for them. How do any of them remind you of God?

Pay attention to the soil, the flowers, the grass, and the concrete. What do they add to your life? If possible, pick a blade of grass or a flower. What makes it beautiful? How do these things remind you of God?

The next time you are at the beach or get a glass of water, just observe the water. Touch it. What about the water makes you feel happy? What would life be like without water? How does water remind you of God?

Pets have a way of loving us unconditionally. We often have to care for our pets and give them more attention than we would human beings. What about your pet do you like? How does your pet bring you closer to God? How does your pet help you enjoy your life?

Get a blank piece of paper and study it at various times throughout the day. What does its blankness or emptiness make you think of? How does this blank sheet of paper make you feel? How does it remind you of God?

The next time you are in church, spend a few moments noticing all the objects. A church may have many ornaments as a means of enhancing worship. What in the church appeals to you and makes you feel closer to God? Which is your favorite stained-glass window? Why? What in your church makes you feel comfortable? Keep that image in mind. Pray, and ask God to use you in the same way that the object is used in church.

Shapes are a great means of helping the mind come closer to certain realities. Circles, squares, rectangles, and triangles have special uses and significance. How does the shape you like teach you about God? How does it remind you of God? Pray to be like that the shape you chose.

Walk a labyrinth. This is a great way to calm the soul and meditate. If you cannot make it to a labyrinth, go for a "holy" walk. Repeat the Jesus prayer (Jesus, Son of the living God, have mercy on me), or invite the Spirit to show you new things about God as you walk.

What do you like about your school or your work? Who there makes you happy? Who reminds you most of God? How does your work or school bring you closer to God?

Light a candle, and just sit in silence looking at it. How does the light remind you about God?

Create or make something. How does creating something remind you about God?

Embodied Prayer
My wife, Kathy, and I have developed this form of prayer based on our work with Chinese gurus and with friends.

Option A
1. Begin by closing your eyes. Stand with your feet shoulder-width apart. Bend your knees slightly.
2. Begin to quiet down and follow your breathing. Focus on your inhale and exhale. *[Pause]*
3. Now begin to shake your arms and legs wildly.
4. Shake out all the tensions of the week, of the commute, everything.
5. Continue to shake for another minute.
6. When you are ready, add a sound, a sigh. Breathe out all negativity, doubt, distraction.
7. Slowly come to a stop with the shaking, and rest your arms loosely at your sides.
8. Feel the energy radiating from your body.
9. Imagine it radiating out into the circle and touching all of us in the circle. *[Rest there for a moment.]*

Option B
1. Slowly bring your hands together and cup them, as if you were holding a small bird.
2. Raise your hands to the level of your heart, and hold them about six inches away from your heart.
3. Feel your heart filling with loving kindness, growing outward so that it reaches your cupped hands.
4. Continue to grow the compassionate energy in your heart. Feel the radiance growing.

5. Now imagine that you are opening the gates to your heart, and with your hands, slowly extend that compassionate energy into the center of the circle.
6. Then extend your arms out from your sides, radiating compassionate energy to all of us here. Feel the energy of the group. And rest there. *[Pause]*

Option C

1. Very slowly raise your arms over your head and gather a ball of light at the top of your crown. Visualize the healing power of the Holy Spirit between your hands.
2. Slowly pull that healing power down into your brain. Feel it washing your brain, exposing what is wise and what is true.
3. Now pull that healing power down through your body center—very slowly, pausing at each point.
4. Feel its energy washing your body.
5. Through your face.
6. Through your throat.
7. Through your heart.
8. Through your solar plexus.
9. Through your belly.
10. Through your pelvis.
11. And down the fronts of your legs.
12. Now, just stand and abide in the radiance of the Spirit's healing power.
13. Then extend your arms out from your sides, to extend the healing power to those of us here today.

Keep praying.